United States
Department of
Agriculture

Forest Service

Pacific Northwest
Research Station

General Technical Report
PNW-GTR-858

January 2012

Forage Resource Evaluation System for Habitat—Deer: An Interactive Deer Habitat Model

Thomas A. Hanley, Donald E. Spalinger, Kenrick J. Mock, Oran L. Weaver, and Grant M. Harris

Authors

Thomas A. Hanley is a research wildlife biologist, U.S. Department of Agriculture, Forest Service, Pacific Northwest Research Station, Forestry Sciences Laboratory, 11305 Glacier Highway, Juneau, AK 99801-8626. **Donald E. Spalinger** is a professor, Department of Biology, and **Kenrick J. Mock** is an associate professor, Department of Mathematical Sciences, University of Alaska Anchorage, 3211 Providence Drive, Anchorage, AK 99508-4614. **Oran L. Weaver** is a contract computer programmer who lives in Anchorage, AK. **Grant M. Harris** was a wildlife ecologist, U.S. Department of Agriculture, Forest Service, Chugach National Forest, 3301 C Street, Suite 300, Anchorage, AK 99503-3998. Harris is currently a chief of the biology division with the Southwest Region of the U.S. Fish and Wildlife Service, 500 Gold Street SW, Albuquerque, NM 87103.

Cover photographs by Miles Hemstrom and Tom Iraci.

Abstract

Hanley, Thomas A.; Spalinger, Donald E.; Mock, Kenrick J.; Weaver, Oran L.; Harris, Grant M. 2012. Forage resource evaluation system for habitat—deer: an interactive deer habitat model. Gen. Tech. Rep. PNW-GTR-858. Portland, OR: U.S. Department of Agriculture, Forest Service, Pacific Northwest Research Station. 64 p.

We describe a food-based system for quantitatively evaluating habitat quality for deer called the Forage Resource Evaluation System for Habitat and provide its rationale and suggestions for use. The system was developed as a tool for wildlife biologists and other natural resource managers and planners interested in evaluating habitat quality and, especially, comparing two or more patches of habitat or the same patch at different seasons or under different conditions. It is based on the quantity (of biomass) and quality (digestible energy and digestible protein) of the habitat's food resources in relation to user-specified metabolic requirements of deer (which differ with species, age, sex, season, and reproductive status). It uses a linear programming algorithm to determine the suitable forage that can sustain deer at the specified requirements. Output includes the number of deer days (1 deer day equals one deer for 1 day) per unit area that the available food resources are capable of supporting, the species composition of the solution set to the linear programming problem, and the relative importance of biomass versus nutritional quality as limiting factors of the habitat for deer. The system is accessed via the Internet (http://cervid.uaa.alaska.edu/deer/home.aspx) and consists of a Web-based application for analysis at the patch (or "stand") scale and a geographical information system (GIS)-based application for analysis at the landscape scale, which includes spatial effects of patch sizes and their shapes and locations in relation to deer home ranges. Although the system was developed for Sitka black-tailed deer (*Odocoileus hemionus sitkensis*) in southeastern Alaska and illustrated with examples for them, it also can be applied for other species of deer (with the exception of very large species such as moose, *Alces alces*) elsewhere in the world.

Keywords: Black-tailed deer, *Odocoilius hemionus*, Alaska, habitat evaluation, carrying capacity, nutrition, forest planning.

Contents

1 **Overview of the Forage Resource Evaluation System for Habitat**

1 Introduction

6 Linear Programming Model

7 Factors Affecting Nutrition and Palatability

11 Carrying Capacity Models

14 Two Calculators: Stand-Level Application and Landscape-Level Application

16 Different Deer (Cervidae) Species

16 Current Status and Future Plans

17 **FRESH-Deer for Sitka Black-Tailed Deer in Alaska—Example**

18 Focal Species and Habitat

19 Linked Databases

20 Energy and Protein Constraints

22 Other Foraging Constraints, Optional

23 Importance of Variation in Nutritional Values and Habitat Biomass Values

25 Summer to Winter Conversion

28 Snow Submodel

32 Interpretation of Output

34 Home Range

35 User's Manuals

35 **Management Implications**

38 **Acknowledgments**

39 **English Equivalents**

40 **Literature Cited**

48 **Appendix 1: Suggested Field and Laboratory Methods for Obtaining Original Data for Forage Biomass and Nutritional Quality**

53 **Appendix 2: Nutritional Data (Mean ± Standard Deviation) in the Nutritional Database**

58 **Appendix 3: Plant Codes of Species in the Current (2011) Database and Their Default Values for Percentage Remaining in Winter, and Maximum Percentage in the Solution Set**

62 **Glossary**

Overview of the Forage Resource Evaluation System for Habitat

Introduction

The Forage Resource Evaluation System for Habitat (FRESH) is a system for evaluating habitat quality for deer (family Cervidae) on the basis of available food, its nutritional quality, and the nutritional requirements of deer. The FRESH system has been available to the public on the Internet via a University of Alaska Anchorage Web site[1] (http://cervid.uaa.alaska.edu/deer/home.aspx) since 2005. It was designed with adult female Sitka black-tailed deer (*Odocoileus hemionus sitkensis*) in Alaska as the prototype, but it can be used for other medium-size deer (Cervidae) species elsewhere in the world. We focus on food because it clearly sets the potential upper limit on the number of animals a habitat can support. Forage resources (vegetation and nutritional quality) can be measured in the field and can be manipulated by land management. We focus on **digestible energy**[2] and **digestible protein**, because they are the two most common nutritional limiting factors for wild ungulates (Moen 1973, Short 1981, White 1993), and their requirements are reasonably well known for black-tailed deer and other cervids (Robbins 1993). We focus on adult females because they are the productive segment of the population, the animals that produce young. Nutritional requirements vary seasonally and with reproductive status (e.g., body maintenance without young versus gestation or lactation requirements). This system is suitable for any habitat and any species of medium-size deer where the availability of forage, its nutritional quality, and the nutritional requirements of the deer are known.

The analytical system provides a "snapshot" analysis at one user-specified point in time. It is assumed that all available vegetation is potential food, and there is no accounting for long-term herbivore-plant dynamics (e.g., the effects of overbrowsing). This is not a simulation model. Rather, it is a calculator: given specific values of available forage **biomass**, its nutritional quality, and animal requirements, it calculates the maximum number of "**animal days**" (one adult female for 1 day) that can be sustained by the forage resource. The animal day values are best considered in a relative (comparative) sense, not as absolute values, because they are the maximum number of animal days (at one point in time) that can be supported by the food if all the suitable food were eaten then (no herbivore-plant **feedback loops**).

---

[1] Although implemented on the University of Alaska Web site in 2005, the FRESH system might eventually move to a Forest Service Web site but remain accessible to the general public.

[2] See Glossary for terms highlighted in bold at first mention.

The snapshot values from our model are valid for only their point of measurement and analysis; they are not an annual, or even seasonal, average.

The instantaneous, food-based "**carrying capacity**" (see box 1) of an actual habitat varies continuously (fig. 1) with marked changes in **plant phenology** and diet (fig. 2) and animal **metabolic requirements** (see box 2) during summer and with variation in snowpack during winter. The snapshot values from our model are valid for only their point of measurement and analysis; they are not an annual, or even seasonal, average. They are best used for comparing two or more habitats, or the same habitat(s) in two or more states (times or post-manipulation, succession, etc.). Additionally, a large-scale, geographic information system (GIS) application of the system is useful for comparing patterns within the same landscape or various landscapes—where size and spatial configuration of habitats are important considerations.

Box 1: Carrying Capacity

We define "carrying capacity" as the number of "animal days"* per unit area that a given habitat can support, based on the quantity and quality of its food resources. We do not account for dynamic herbivore-plant interactions (e.g., overgrazing, "proper-use factors," **feedback loops**, subsequent effects on plant growth, etc.). We base our calculations on the total supply of plant biomass ("current annual growth"—see box 3, p. 8) that is "available" (see box 4, p. 8) to the animal species in question. We are essentially answering the question, "If one were to harvest all of the available current annual growth of plants in a given area and bring it into a captive animal facility, how many animal days could the food support while meeting a user-specified level of "metabolic requirements" (see box 2, p. 5)?" The animal days are always specified by the user's choice of metabolic requirements. We usually work with adult females as the "animal," and we specify their reproductive status (i.e., maintenance, reproductive, etc.—see metabolic requirements box 2, p 5). Adult females are the productive segment of the population of deer, and their nutritional status is a very useful criterion for evaluating range condition or carrying capacity.

We usually work with spatial units of 1 ha. Thus, we work with "animal days per hectare."

Notice that our definition of carrying capacity is a "snap-shot" definition, applied to one particular point in time—the time when plant biomass and nutritional quality have been measured. However, the user should be aware that plant biomass, nutritional quality, and metabolic requirements change continuously throughout the year.

* One animal day is the food necessary to support one animal for one day at the specified level of nutrition. For example, 22 animal days could be one animal for 22 days, or 22 animals for one day, or any combination thereof.

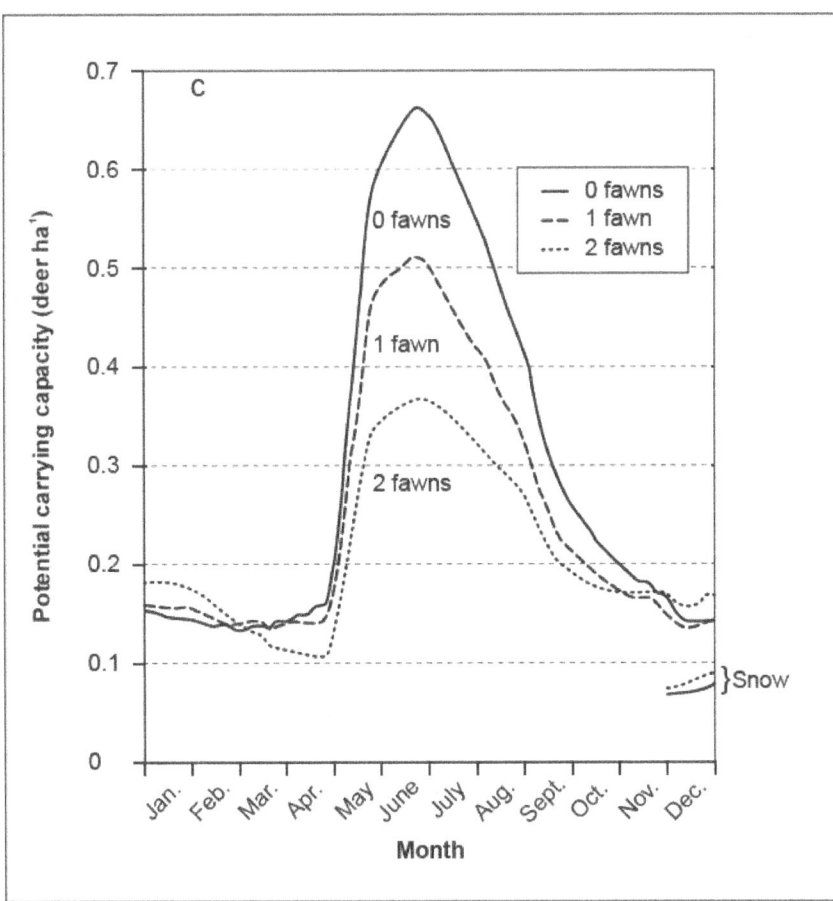

Figure 1—Monthly changes in potential carrying capacity (deer/ha/year) at one study site on Admiralty Island, southeastern Alaska; all values are for snow-free conditions, except those shown for December with a depth of 20 cm. (Source: Hanley and McKendrick 1985.)

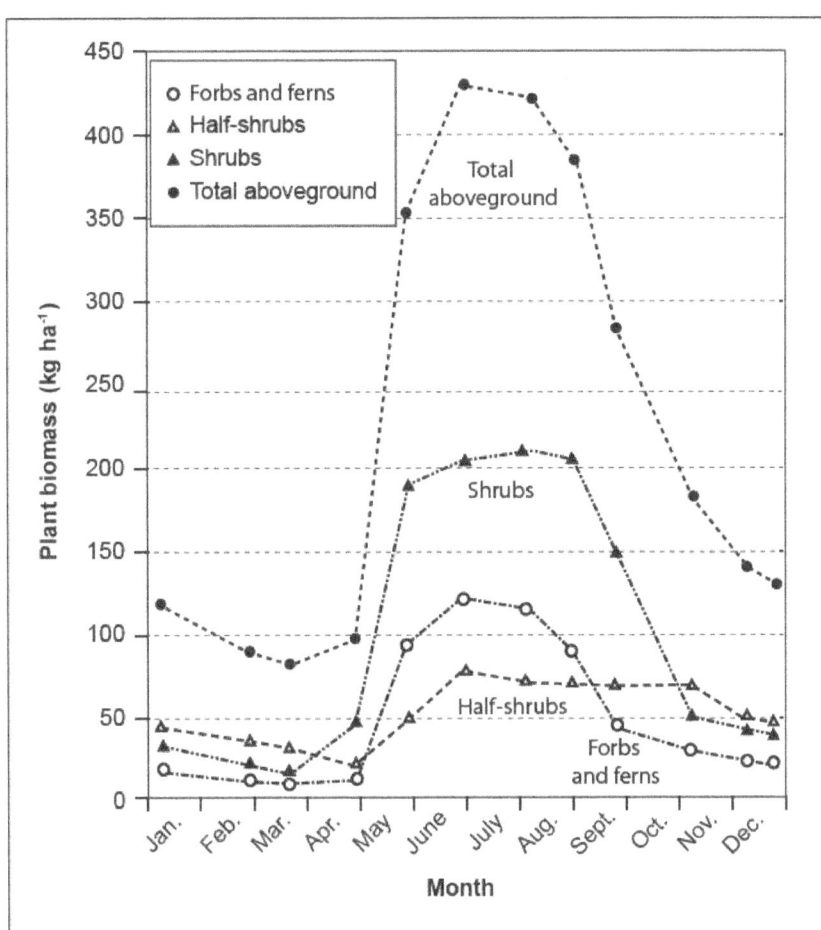

Figure 2a—Monthly changes in plant biomass (current annual growth), January–December 1981, Admiralty Island, Alaska. Values for January and December were estimated by extrapolating between November and February. All values reflect the availability of plant biomass in the absence of snow. Total aboveground values include conifer seedlings and litter, lichens, and mushrooms. (Source: Hanley and McKendrick 1985.)

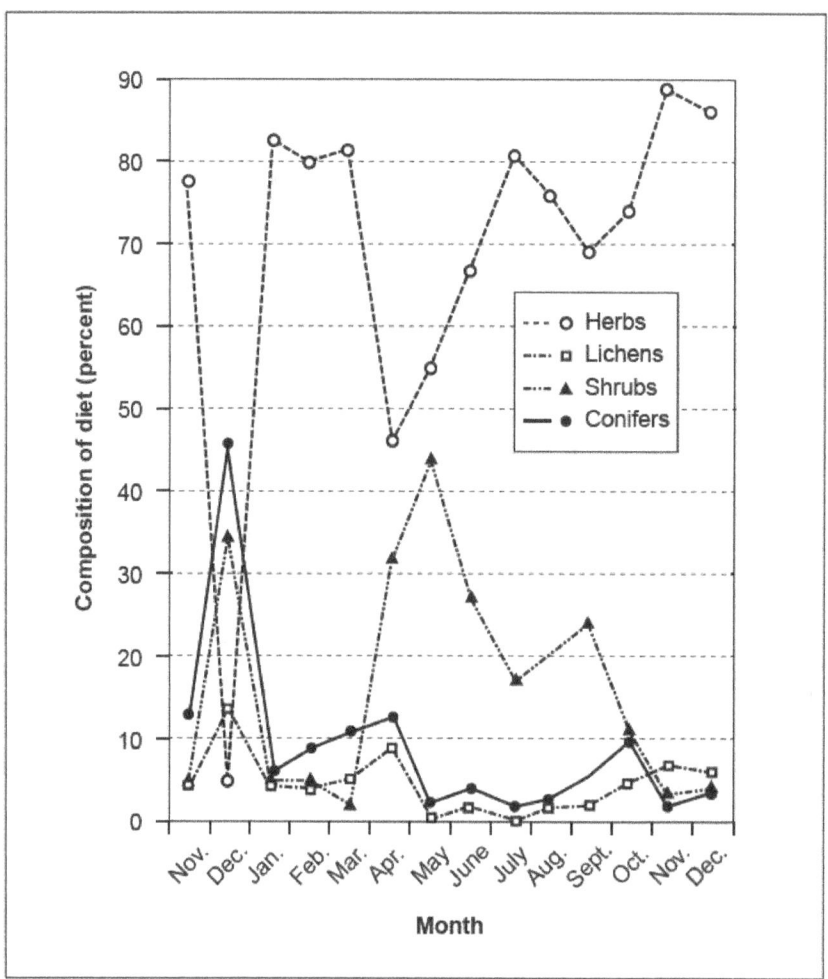

Figure 2b—Estimated monthly diet composition, November 1980–December 1981, Admiralty Island, Alaska. Values are based on fecal composition data adjusted for in vitro dry-matter digestibility (Hanley and McKendrick 1983, Rochelle 1980 for lichens). Values for January and December 1981 were estimated by extrapolating between November and February 1981. Only values for December 1980 reflect the presence of snow. "Herbs" is the combined categories of "forbs and ferns" and "half-shrubs." (Source: Hanley and McKendrick 1985.)

The FRESH system includes linked databases of understory biomass and forage-specific nutritional data for a variety of habitats and forages. The databases provide the user with examples or reference points (in the case of habitats) and ballpark-level default estimates (in the case of forages) for data that the user might not have. Although field data obtained directly from the user's study area always are best, a user can use FRESH to explore habitat relations with estimates of vegetation or habitat variables based on the examples and default values from the linked databases stored within FRESH.

Box 2: Metabolic Requirements

Our model runs on user-specified requirements for metabolizable energy and protein. It also requires a user-specified daily rate of dry-matter intake of food (**ovendry weight** of total food intake in a day). These values are empirically determined. We have provided a recommended set of metabolic requirements for Sitka black-tailed deer (see table 1, p. 21) based on scientific literature, although the user can choose different values if they have a sound basis for doing so. Carrying capacity (see box 1 and Glossary) values will differ dramatically, depending on user-specified metabolic requirements. This is a very important consideration in any evaluation of habitat, as summer range is very different than winter range, and habitat suitable for only "maintenance" levels in summer may have much lower carrying capacities at "reproductive" levels.

Metabolic requirements of animals differ greatly seasonally and as a function of age, sex, reproductive status, and body condition. Summer is a time of growth, body reserve accumulation, and reproduction (lactation). Winter is a time of growth stasis, weight loss, and deterioration of body condition (catabolism of reserves). We usually work with adult females as our unit for analysis (see box 3, p. 8). Summer metabolic requirements for adult females depend on their body condition going into summer, their reproductive status (maintenance only, or maintenance plus lactation for one or more fawns), and their need to accumulate body reserves (fat and protein) before going into winter. Winter metabolic requirements depend on the animal's body condition (reserves) going into winter and their activity levels (or winter weather) influencing the rate at which they draw on their energy reserves—with the difference between the two (reserves minus draw-down) needing to be made up by food resources.

Our recommended set of metabolic requirements (table 1) for summer includes lactation requirements for both single and twin fawns. However, the values are for peak lactation requirements, not "average" requirements across the entire summer. Peak requirements are relatively high, and peak requirements for twin fawns are especially high. Peak requirements can be met by the adult female through a combination of using her own body reserves and relying on food intake. Thus, peak requirements, especially for twin fawns, might be an unreasonably high standard for evaluating carrying capacity of a habitat. Therefore, we usually use the recommended requirements for "single fawn" and refer to that as simply "reproduction" (unspecified as to singletons

(*continued on next page*)

or twins). Of course, the user can specify whatever they wish for these requirements.

Our recommended set of metabolic requirements (table 1) for winter includes two alternatives, depending upon the user-assumed body condition of the animals going into winter: one set of requirements is for "fat" animals coming off high-quality summer range; the other set is for "lean" animals coming off poor-quality summer range. "Fat" animals have greater body reserves than do "lean" animals, and therefore have lower requirements from their food resources to survive the winter. Our "requirements" are the requirements from the food resources. We assume similar activity budgets, winter weather conditions, and appetites (dry-matter intake rates) for both alternatives.

Metabolic requirements can be specified in terms of digestible energy (in kilocalories or kilojoules), dry-matter digestibility of the diet (percentage of dry matter), digestible protein (percentage of dry matter), or crude protein (percentage of dry matter). The choices must be specified by the user. Use of either digestible energy or digestible dry matter (both relate to metabolizable energy requirement) includes an assumed constant metabolic energy coefficient; use of dry-matter digestibility of the diet includes a further assumed constant gross energy content of all forages. Protein requirements are dealt with by digestible protein or crude protein. Digestible protein includes effects of plant **tannins** on reducing protein digestibility. Crude protein does not include effects of tannins and should be viewed as highly suspect—although, often times, tannin effects are unknown and only data for crude protein are available.

Linear Programming Model

The calculation of animal days follows from an earlier, iterative procedure (Hanley and Rogers 1989) that expanded on theory first proposed by Hobbs and Swift (1985). It is now accomplished with a linear programming model. Linear programming models are optimization algorithms, where an objective is maximized (or minimized) within a set of maximum or minimum constraints. They are called linear programming models because they consist of a series of equations, each of which is written as a linear equation (e.g., $Y > a + bc + de + fg$), and the solution is found by solving all equations simultaneously. In our case, the objective that is to be maximized is the quantity of forage biomass (kilograms per hectare [kg/ha] or pounds per acre [lb/ac]) that can be pooled from all available biomass while meeting (or exceeding) specified minimum constraints for digestible energy and digestible protein. We are essentially answering the question, "If one were to harvest all the available **current annual growth** of plants in a given area and bring it into a captive animal facility for feeding, what is the maximum number of animal days that could be supported while meeting (or exceeding) user-specified levels of metabolic requirements (mean concentration of digestible energy and digestible protein)?" We answer that question by using a linear programming model to determine the maximum amount of forage biomass that can be pooled (from the combination of all available forages) while meeting the specified constraints.[3] The maximum suitable biomass (kg/ha) is then divided by the user-specified daily dry-matter intake of an adult female (kg/day), yielding the maximum number of animal days (days/ha) that can be supported within the specified constraints.

The data-entry requirements for analyzing any given habitat are the following: (1) a list of all available "forages" (See boxes 3 and 4; a forage is a plant part with a unique nutritional composition—e.g., different species are different forages; shrub leaves are different forages from shrub twigs, even within the same species); (2) the available biomass (kg/ha, dry weight) of each forage; (3) the concentration of digestible energy (kilojoules per gram [kJ/g]) of each forage; (4) the concentration of digestible protein (percentage of dry weight) of each forage; (5) the daily energy requirement (kJ/day) of an adult female; the daily digestible protein requirement (grams per day [g/day]) of an adult female; and the daily dry-matter intake (g/day) of an adult female. We provide guidelines for all the animal data inputs for female black-tailed deer; the forage variables (biomass and nutritional quality) are the chief data requirements from the user (see app. 1 for suggested field and laboratory methods for original data requirements). If the user does not have their own plant nutritional data, they can use our plant nutritional database (automatically linked database) for estimates.

Factors Affecting Nutrition and Palatability

Animal requirements for digestible energy and digestible protein are well known because they are such basic currencies and common limiting factors in animal nutrition, and thus have been studied extensively (National Research Council

> We are essentially answering the question, "If one were to harvest all the available current annual growth of plants in a given area and bring it into a captive animal facility for feeding, what is the maximum number of animal days that could be supported while meeting (or exceeding) user-specified levels of metabolic requirements?"

---

[3] There also is an optional forage-specific constraint limiting the maximum proportion of the solution that can be comprised of the given forage regardless of its digestible energy and digestible protein concentrations (see "Factors Affecting Nutrition and Palatability" section). This is necessary to deal with forages that have high digestible energy, protein, and biomass availability, yet are known to be eaten in only very small quantities.

Box 3: Forages

We consider "forages" to be only the current annual growth of plant species (except for lichens, which are considered whole). Current annual growth is the plant tissue produced in the current year, exclusive of radial growth of older stems in shrubs and belowground growth of all plants. For herbaceous plants, it is the total aboveground biomass. For shrubs and trees, it is the current year's twigs and leaves. Current annual growth is almost always of much higher nutritional quality than is older growth (dead, previous year's herbaceous material and older shrub or tree stems); in fact, the older growth is usually of such low nutritional quality that we do not consider it "food." However, the user can choose to include whatever they wish as food. For example, if old stems are included, estimates of their energy and protein values must be included, and it is important to consider them separately from current year's twigs because the nutritional values differ greatly.

Notice that we analyze shrub twigs separately from shrub leaves; i.e., we treat them as different foods, or forages, even though they are the same plant species. This is because the nutritional quality of twigs differs greatly from that of leaves. The choice of what constitutes a separate food, or forage, is entirely up to the user. What is important is that whatever the user's choice for "forage," the biomass and nutritional measures must be made accordingly. If two very different forages (e.g., shrub leaves and twigs, or twigs and old stems) are treated as just one (combined) forage, then the potential roles of those forages will be significantly diluted in the analysis.

Box 4: Available Biomass

"Available biomass" is the plant biomass that is available to the herbivore at the time of the analysis. In summer, it is the total standing crop of current year's growth of a given species of plant. In winter, the available biomass for a given species can be greatly reduced from its summer value by seasonal loss of above-ground tissue (deciduous species) and by burial by snow. Black-tailed deer are not known to paw through snow in search of forage; thus food resources buried by snow are unavailable to deer. Other food resources (e.g., lichens in trees, twigs of very tall shrubs) might be out of reach because they are too high for deer to reach. However, after a snowpack has firmed, especially with a frozen crust, black-tailed deer are able to walk freely on top of the snowpack. Moose are known to "walk down" tall shrubs to reach high portions. The "availability" of any forage is something that the user must consider when inputting the "available" plant biomass into the analysis.

2007, Robbins 1993, Van Soest 1982). Energy is needed for maintaining body heat, fueling activity and growth, and conducting basal metabolic processes. Protein is needed for building and maintaining body tissue. Not all energy and protein consumed by an animal, however, are metabolically available to the animal. "Gross energy" (kJ/g) is the total energy contained in the food—the amount that would be released by combustion. Only the energy in the digestible portion of a food, however, is available to the animal (Robbins 1993). Energy in the indigestible fraction passes from the animal as excretory products (feces, and, to a lesser extent, urine), which are unused. The energy in the digestible fraction is called "digestible energy." Some of that is lost as heat in conversion to "metabolic" energy, but the metabolic energy coefficient for most forages is nearly constant (at about 0.85; Robbins 1993), so we have focused the analysis on digestible energy rather than metabolic energy per se.

Similarly, "crude protein" (which is calculated simply as 6.25 times the total nitrogen concentration of a forage) is only a rough index of the available protein content of a forage. Importantly, the digestible fraction of the protein in forage can vary greatly, especially for wild forages commonly eaten by deer, which may contain tannins and other protein digestion-reducing compounds (Hanley et al. 1992, Robbins et al. 1987a). Thus, the "digestible protein" concentration of forage is much more important than its crude protein concentration when evaluating forages for deer species.

Because digestible energy and digestible protein have been so widely studied, good laboratory analytical techniques exist for measuring or estimating their values in forages, some of them specifically designed for deer (Hanley et al. 1992). For similar reasons, energy and protein requirements of animals, including deer, also are reasonably well known (Robbins 1993). Thus, digestible energy and digestible protein are our most sound currencies for evaluating forage quality for deer (see app. 1 for discussion and details of the importance of choice of methodology for evaluating forage quality).

The nutritional quality of plant material, however, is far more complex than simply digestible energy and digestible protein. Animals also require vitamins, minerals, and micronutrients (National Research Council 2007, Robbins 1993). The bacterial flora in the ruminant stomach of deer synthesizes vitamins, so vitamins are not an important limiting factor (Van Soest 1982). Minerals and micronutrients are important, but usually they are in sufficient concentration in forage, so they are less likely a limiting factor than is energy or protein (Hudson and White 1985, Moen 1973, Robbins 1993). Rarely are levels of minerals or micronutrients inadequate or so abundant as to be toxic. Therefore, mineral and micronutrient requirements of deer species have received much less scientific investigation than have energy and protein, and they are much less understood. We have not included mineral or micronutrient requirements in our analysis, although theoretically they could be added as minimal constraints in an expanded linear programming algorithm.

Moreover, wild forages for herbivores like deer also contain many noxious compounds—some affecting palatability, some affecting digestibility, and some even toxic. Noxious organic compounds abound in wild plants, especially in forbs, ferns, shrubs, and trees—all the forages commonly consumed by deer and other browsers. Ecologists have frequently termed these compounds "**secondary compounds**" or secondary chemistry (secondary to basic plant metabolism) and have considered them as defensive mechanisms protecting plants from herbivory (Rosenthal and Janzen 1979). They are classified in two principal groups differing functionally in the herbivore: (1) digestion-reducing compounds, which decrease the value of forage by decreasing its energy or protein digestibility; and (2) toxins, which produce acute debilitating effects in the herbivore. The two groups are not necessarily exclusive; some compounds serve both functions. Deer actually eat many forages with high levels of secondary compounds by mixing them in small amounts in a highly diverse diet. Plant secondary chemistry (the study of secondary compounds) is an enormously complex subject, with thousands of compounds in the environment and different compounds in virtually every forage. The effects of one major class of compounds (tannins) have been studied well enough to be incorporated into laboratory analytical techniques for estimating digestible energy and digestible protein (Robbins et al. 1987a, 1987b, 1991), but the effects of most compounds are largely unknown. Plant secondary chemistry is far too complex to model at this time, yet it has very real effects on herbivore use of plants—either through learned behavior or through innate palatability preferences/avoidances of specific forages. As explained below, we deal with this problem by calculating the effects of tannins on digestible protein and digestible dry matter (Hanley et al. 1992) and by allowing the user to specify limits on the amount of unpalatable foods that are suitable for the solution to the linear programming problem.

"Nutritional wisdom" (the ability of animals to select their food on the basis of its nutritional value) is an old hypothesis, yet it has never satisfactorily explained diet choice by herbivores in natural settings. Palatability of forages and diet selection in large herbivores are far more complex than simply the nutritional value of the food (Gillingham et al. 1997; Hanley 1997; Spalinger and Robbins 1992; Spalinger et al. 1986, 1993). Plant secondary chemistry complicates the problem even further. We must acknowledge that forage quality is more than simply digestible energy and digestible protein (Parker et al. 1996), and we must account for the fact that some forages are avoided (unpalatable) despite high levels of digestible energy and digestible protein. But we must do this within a relatively simple model.

We have taken a very pragmatic approach to the solution of "unpalatability"— the problem of apparently good forages (in terms of digestible energy and protein) not being eaten or eaten in only small proportions, despite abundant availability, e.g., alder (*Alnus* spp.). Forages like alder pose a significant problem in the linear programming solution, because the solution would include much or all of the alder and, therefore, would inflate the apparent value of the habitat beyond its true value. Our approach to resolving this problem in a simple, pragmatic way is to add additional, forage-specific constraints to the linear programming model, whereby an upper limit (maximum constraint) can be specified for each forage known to be relatively unpalatable, regardless of its digestible energy and protein concentrations. Thus, if 3.0 percent is specified as the maximum constraint for alder, for example, then that will be the maximum amount of alder in the linear programming solution. Values for the forage-specific constraints are user-specified. However, the user can base their choice of such values on the results of diet composition studies (e.g., fecal composition or rumen analyses) of deer in similar habitats (e.g., Lewis 1992, 1994; Hanley et al. 1985; Parker et al. 1999; Pierce 1981). Thus, the forage-specific constraint can be based on field data, not just professional opinion (see app. 2 for default values for forages in the current database). This provides a relatively simple and workable solution to a problem that is far too complex to model biologically. In short, the linear programming solution is driven by forage availability, digestible energy, and digestible protein, but it can be restricted by empirically determined limits on palatability of any given forage.

Carrying Capacity Models

The FRESH system is not a carrying capacity model; it is far more limited than that. "Carrying capacity" (see box 1) is an ambiguous term in ecology. It is usually meant to be the maximum number of animals (of a given species) that a given habitat can support indefinitely (Caughley 1977, May 1973, Pielou 1977). The "indefinitely" aspect requires that trophic dynamics (herbivore-plant, predator-prey) be considered and that the system maintains a stable equilibrium for a long (indefinite) time. Carrying capacity is a useful concept for theoretical system modeling, but it is very problematic for practical application. In the real world, virtually no habitat is stable indefinitely, even within "dynamic equilibrium bounds." Seasonal variations occur throughout the year; annual variations occur between years (e.g., weather); and disturbances, succession, and other ecological changes are present over both short and long time scales. "Maximum number of animals" can vary, depending on sex and age composition desired or assumed, as well as expectations for productivity of the population (e.g., "maximum sustained yield" versus "maximum sustained density") (Caughley 1977, Hobbs 1989, McCullough 1979).

In practical application, carrying capacity is best determined empirically, after carefully defining exactly what is meant about location, time scale, reasonable limits of natural variation (e.g., are droughts or extreme winters included?), and animal population demographics. This has been done occasionally for closely managed deer populations (McCullough 1979), and it has been done extensively for managing livestock grazing (Stoddart et al. 1975). It requires much empirical experience with the animals and the habitats, including sound data on animal demographics and vegetation dynamics, and usually, careful manipulation of the animal population. Yet, extrapolation to other habitats than those studied involves much uncertainty. For most large, free-ranging populations of deer species, empirical determination of carrying capacity is impossible.

Theoretical calculation or estimation of carrying capacity for large herbivores is confounded by two major problems: (1) food quantity and quality are not substitutable for one another (Hobbs 1989, Hobbs and Hanley 1990, Wallmo et al. 1977); and (2) the diet selection process, central to predicting diet composition, has remained an exceedingly difficult process to model or predict (Hanley 1997), especially for a novel vegetation. The combination of these two problems has implications well beyond estimating carrying capacity on the basis of food supplies. It also confounds the interpretation of results from habitat-use studies (e.g., habitat selection or preferences) and models of habitat quality derived from such data (e.g., "resource utilization functions") (Hobbs and Hanley 1990, Van Horne 1983).

The problem of "nonsubstitutability" of quantity and quality of food is that poor quality food cannot be substituted for deficiencies of high-quality food—i.e., much poor food is not equal to less good food. The reason is that herbivores are limited by the amount of food that they can process (i.e., ingest, digest, and pass through their digestive tract). When they reach their limit of intake, they cannot consume more; they cannot make up for poor quality food by eating more of it. In fact, food intake usually decreases with decreasing food quality (e.g., Cook et al. 2004, White 1983). The most common cause is bulk-passage limitations through the gastrointestinal tract (especially problematic for ruminants, with their four-chambered stomach) (Spalinger et al. 1986, 1993; Spalinger and Robbins 1992). Thus, one cannot simply multiply the biomass of forages by their digestible energy (or protein) concentrations, sum for all forages, and then divide by the animal's daily metabolic requirement to determine the number of animal days that the food can sustain (Wallmo et al. 1977). Furthermore, virtually every forage in the habitat is unique—it has a unique combination of biomass and nutritional quality. Thus, it is the combination (mix) of forages that must be optimized in order to quantify the quality of a habitat's food resources. Some of the potential foods may or may not be suitable, depending on what else and how much of it is in the diet and the nutritional requirements of the animal.

Empirical observations of diet composition of free-ranging herbivores provide a way of determining a suitable mix of potential foods. Some models of carrying capacity apply empirically observed diet composition to the array of potential foods in the habitat to determine the maximum quantity of food that can be mixed in that same proportion (Hobbs 1989). The problem with this is that diet composition is not a static, fixed attribute of an animal-habitat interaction. It differs with the relative availabilities of the various foods, and therefore, differs with animal population density as well. As population density increases, for example, the most preferred foods decrease in availability, and diet composition shifts, yet the habitat still might yield a diet that is well above minimal requirements. This is the similar problem with habitat-use studies—habitat preferences (and resource utilization functions), should be expected to shift with changes in relative availabilities of habitats in a landscape and with population densities of the animal, the latter because food quantity and quality are not substitutable for one another (Hobbs and Hanley 1990). The best habitats for an individual animal when population densities are low may be those that provide low quantities of high-quality food. At higher population densities, however, such habitats may not provide enough food, and more animals may choose a habitat that provides a higher quantity of lower (but sufficient) quality food—i.e., exactly the opposite pattern of habitat preference. An accurate diet prediction model ("optimal foraging theory") would enable us to account for the interaction of forage availability, nutritional quality, and herbivore population density; but no such model exists as yet for ruminants, as interactive complexities abound (Hanley 1997).

We have taken a very pragmatic approach to resolving this dilemma by avoiding the prediction of diet composition altogether; similarly, we do not predict habitat preference or use, either. Instead, we move directly to the question, "what is the maximum number of animals (or animal days) that can be supported by a given food resource at a given level of metabolic requirement?" Our answer is the maximum number of animal days that can be supported at that instant of analysis (the time when food supplies were measured), without concern for an "indefinite" or "stable" concept of carrying capacity (herbivore-plant interactions) or the composition of diets at anything less than the maximum density of animals. We calculate

It is the combination (mix) of forages that must be optimized in order to quantify the quality of a habitat's food resources. Some of the potential foods may or may not be suitable, depending on what else and how much of it is in the diet and the nutritional requirements of the animal.

the dietary mix that solves the optimization problem of the linear program: maximize the quantity of suitable forage biomass within the specified minimum constraints of digestible energy concentration and digestible protein concentration, and maximum, forage-specific limits for forages known to be unpalatable. Our solution would be the "optimal diet" only at that population density that is the maximum for the habitat, and it would be optimal only for the population as a whole, not for the individual animal, which is where diet choices are made. This is not a diet prediction model; it is an animal feeding capacity calculator. It is something more akin to what a feedlot manager would use than to what an ecologist would find exciting.

Two Calculators: Stand-Level Application and Landscape-Level Application

The FRESH system has two levels of application—(1) a Web-based, stand-level application; and (2) a GIS-based, landscape-level application. The Web-based application runs on a server. The user imports their stand-level data, or types it in directly, or accesses stand-level data from our linked database. Typical uses might be comparison of results from silviculture treatments, or before-versus-after treatment, or various types of old-growth forests, or various levels of metabolic requirements, etc. Data are analyzed for one stand or habitat—one array of forage availability—at a time.

Where landscape pattern of habitats is an important consideration, the GIS-based application is needed. For example, elevation of any given habitat patch is very important in a landscape analysis of winter range. Also, the juxtaposition of two habitats differing in their food limitations (e.g., one with high-quality food but a low quantity of it, the other with low-quality food and a lot of it) can provide a higher combined carrying capacity than simply the sum of the carrying capacities of the two habitats individually, because high-quality forages from the one habitat can be combined with lower quality forages of the other habitat, thereby making greater overall use of the lower quality foods.

The GIS application is downloaded from the Web site directly onto the user's computer; the user must supply their own GIS data set; and then all calculations take place on the user's computer. The user must have a description of the forage resources (species-specific biomass and nutritional quality) and overstory canopy cover of each habitat type in the landscape. The habitat types must be mapped in the GIS system (ASCII [American Standard Code for Information Interchange] text version of a raster-based vegetation cover and Digital Elevation Model), as elevation must be mapped to help account for snow in winter analyses. Additionally, the user must specify a mean home-range size (hectares [ha]) for the animal (see "Home Range" section). This is a stand-alone GIS application that does not run in ArcMap.

The FRESH system works by analyzing all cells within a moving window (or kernel) the size of the mean home range by computing available forage after accounting for habitat type, elevation, and burial by snow (if in winter). It compiles all available forage within the home range into one composite array of available forage, then uses the same linear programming algorithm as in the stand-level application to calculate an animal-days/ha value for that "home range." It then moves over, by a user-specified amount of space, to another, overlapping area of home range, and repeats the process (an iterative kernel, "moving window" analysis). Hence, each grid cell of the landscape has an array of animal-days/ha values, with each value representing the results of a given iteration for each time that cell occurs in a window. For example, imagine that 50 grid cells representing three different habitat types (each with a different set of forages) occur in a window. One combined array of available forage is calculated as the weighted mean of the habitats in that window, and the maximum number of animal-days/ha that the combined forages can support (based on the linear programming model) is calculated. That value is then assigned to each grid cell within that home range window, regardless of its habitat type. The window then moves over by a user-specified amount, and the process is repeated. Some of the cells will occur in the new window, so they will receive another animal-days/ha value. After the entire landscape has been analyzed in this manner, the mean value of animal-days/ha for each individual grid cell on the landscape is calculated across all of the times that cell occurred in a widow. Thus, each cell has a mean value in relation to the various "home ranges" (windows) in which it occurred, and the mean value of all cells in the full landscape provides an average value for the whole landscape relative to the spatial distribution of its habitat patches. This process accounts for the size and spatial locations of each habitat within a scale appropriate for the animal—its home range. The underlying assumption is that every animal knows an area the size of its home range and can mix forages from anywhere within that home range. The synergistic effect of combining forages from different habitats can be greater than the sum of the values of each habitat considered in isolation. However, the combination of habitats must occur at the scale of what an individual animal knows (i.e., its home range) because diet composition and nutritional requirements operate at the scale of the individual animal.

Typical uses of the GIS-based application might be comparisons of landscape-level management areas, or the same area under various potential management alternatives, or temporal patterns for a landscape as it changes with plant succession or land management treatments. Data are analyzed for all stands in the landscape, all within the same run, and all at the same point of time.

The synergistic effect of combining forages from different habitats can be greater than the sum of the values of each habitat considered in isolation. However, the combination of habitats must occur at the scale of what an individual animal knows (i.e., its home range) because diet composition and nutritional requirements operate at the scale of the individual animal.

Different Deer (Cervidae) Species

The FRESH system can be applied to any medium-size (e.g., 30 to 125 kg) species of large, generalist herbivore (i.e., herbivores that consume a mixed-species diet without specializing on one or a few forages) for which nutritional requirements are reasonably well known and food resources can be quantified. It can be applied anywhere. If additional constraints are needed (e.g., concerning micronutrient limitation in a particular locale), then FRESH cannot be applied directly. Its theoretical basis would still be applicable, but the system would need to be modified to incorporate the new constraint(s). Alternatively, the user could use the current FRESH system by substituting the new constraint(s) for either digestible energy or digestible protein or both.

The current system has been developed with black-tailed deer in Alaska as the focal species. It could easily be applied to mule deer (*O. h. hemionus*) or white-tailed deer (*O. virginianus*) with only minor adjustments to the metabolic requirements and new, original habitat data for food resources. For some other species of deer, especially very large species like moose (*Alces alces*) or perhaps elk (*Cervus elaphus*), however, FRESH is inadequate without adding an additional constraint involving twig size and foraging time (Shipley and Spalinger 1992; Shipley et al. 1994, 1996). The time constraint and twig-size relations are needed because browse forages consumed by moose often occur as very large twigs, and the size of bite taken while feeding on such twigs involves a tradeoff between nutritional quality and time costs of harvesting. Large bites are more time efficient (g/min) than are small bites (Shipley and Spalinger 1993, Spalinger et al. 1988), but small bites (distal ends of twigs) have higher concentrations of digestible energy and digestible protein than do large bites. Thus, each twig presents an array of opportunity (availability) to the moose. Part of the optimization problem is choosing the appropriate bite size(s) for each twig (browse) species (Hobbs et al. 2003, Spalinger and Hobbs 1992). Of course, forage resources of deer and moose range, and metabolic requirements of deer and moose also differ substantially among the species and habitats. But those are relatively simple matters to adjust through user-specified data input.

Current Status and Future Plans

FRESH-Deer is fully operational at both the stand-level (Web-based) and landscape-level (GIS-based) scales of application. We are currently working with the Tongass National Forest (southeastern Alaska) to increase the range of data in the linked databases for both habitat biomass and forage nutritional quality for Sitka black-tailed deer. We will add data to both databases as they become available. We also anticipate updating and improving documentation and user-guide information periodically.

A FRESH-Moose application remains in the development stage. We anticipate both stand-level and landscape-level applications, but database development for habitats and forages requires more time than is needed for FRESH-Deer, as suitable habitat data for moose ranges have not been collected.

Ultimately, we intend to expand the analytical framework of FRESH to include other factors affecting habitat quality at the landscape scale, beyond forage alone. We will consider the current FRESH food-based estimate of carrying capacity as the maximum potential (upper limit) of the habitat, and then modify that value by the "probability of use" of the habitat, determined from a broad "resource utilization function" model (Long et al. 2009, Manly et al. 1993). In other words, the current, food-based FRESH estimate is the carrying capacity that could be achieved if the habitat were fully acceptable to the animal, whereas the resource utilization function model provides an estimate of probability of use of any given patch (GIS cell) of habitat. Resource utilization functions are calculated from habitat-use data, usually radiotelemetry studies, and are best considered descriptions of observed (past) patterns of use rather than predictions of future patterns. However, when multiple habitat-use data sets are available over a wide geographic area and time period, then a resource utilization function model calculated from a meta-analysis of those data sets might be reasonably robust and offer predictive insight. For example, during the 1980s and 1990s in southeastern Alaska, there were four major radiotelemetry studies of habitat use by black-tailed deer—on Admiralty Island (Schoen and Kirchhoff 1985, 1990), Prince of Wales Island (Yeo and Peek 1992), Heceta Island (Farmer 2002), and Mitkof Island (Doerr et al. 2005). Together, those studies cover a broad range of southeastern Alaska over a nearly 20-year period. Resource utilization functions that are consistent across all four studies are likely robust for most of southeastern Alaska's islands and for deer population densities and winters similar to those of the past three decades.

The combination of a food-based upper limit and a behavior-based probability of use should yield interesting insights into habitat value for deer. Also, the differences between the two should be insightful as well.

FRESH-Deer for Sitka Black-Tailed Deer in Alaska—Example

Here we provide the details of the FRESH-Deer system within the context of the species and habitat for which it was developed. Text refers directly to the FRESH-Deer system on the University of Alaska Anchorage Web site (http://cervid.uaa.alaska.edu/deer/Home.aspx).

Focal Species and Habitat

Our system for deer has been designed for Sitka black-tailed deer in southeastern Alaska (Hanley et al. 1989, Parker et al. 1999). The system would work for any similar-size deer anywhere, but the data in our linked databases, recommended metabolic requirements, and snow submodel are all centered on Sitka black-tails and their habitat in Alaska. We focus on the adult female segment of the population, but other segments (e.g., males, yearlings, etc.) could be the focal point by simply specifying appropriate metabolic requirements as the "animal data" constraints.

We recommend focusing on the month of July for summer analysis and field data collection. July is the time of both peak forage biomass and peak nutritional requirements of female deer (fig. 3). Although the user can specify lactation requirements for more than one fawn, such requirements are very high at their peak and tend to produce relatively restrictive results in the analysis. Lactating can draw on some of their own body reserves to get through the peak. Therefore, we usually run the analysis with lactation requirements for one fawn and simply call it

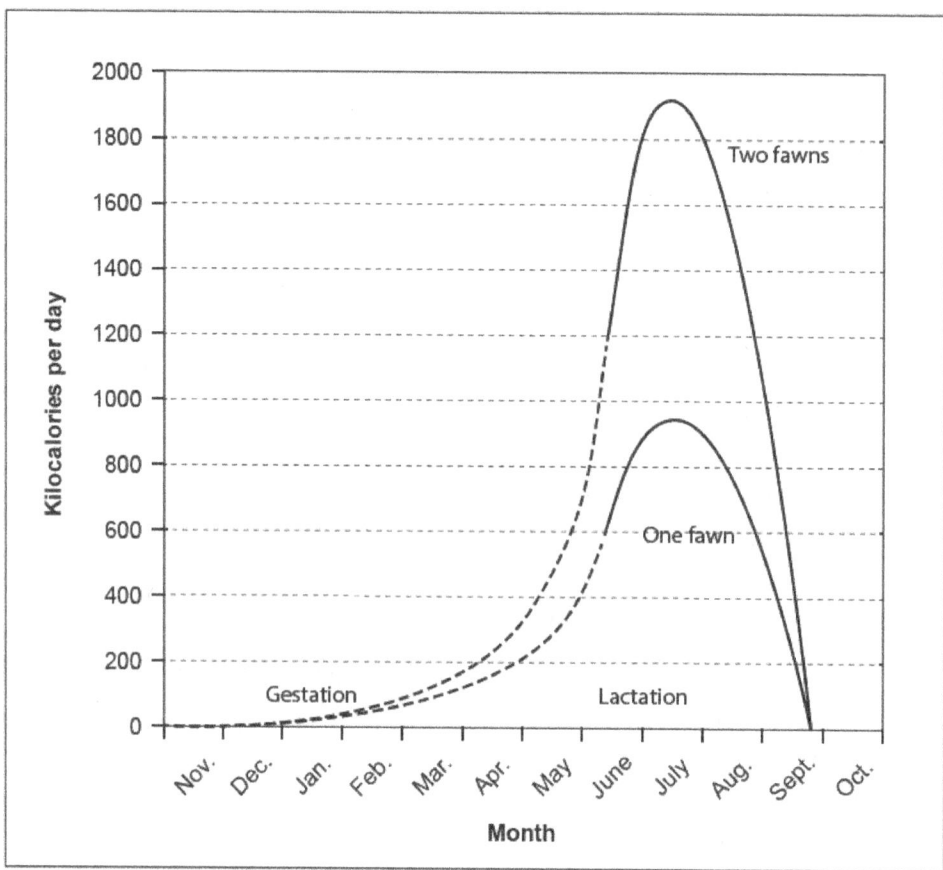

Figure 3—Energy costs (kilocalories/day) of gestation and lactation for a black-tailed deer doe with one or two fawns. (Source: Hanley 1984, based on data from Moen 1973 and Robbins and Moen 1975.)

"reproduction." Requirements for twin fawns, however, can yield further insight into forage nutritional quality of a habitat.

For winter analyses, we have focused on the date of 1 February in the snow submodel of FRESH-Deer (see below). Forage nutritional quality does not change much during winter, but forage availability changes greatly depending on snowpack. Users can choose whatever date they want, but we recommend that they focus on their assumptions about snowpack if choosing a different date than 1 February.

Linked Databases

We provide two databases (forage biomass by habitat and forage nutritional values) that are linked to each other and to user-specified, habitat data entry. The habitat database contains forage-specific biomass data (fig. 4) for forest stands in

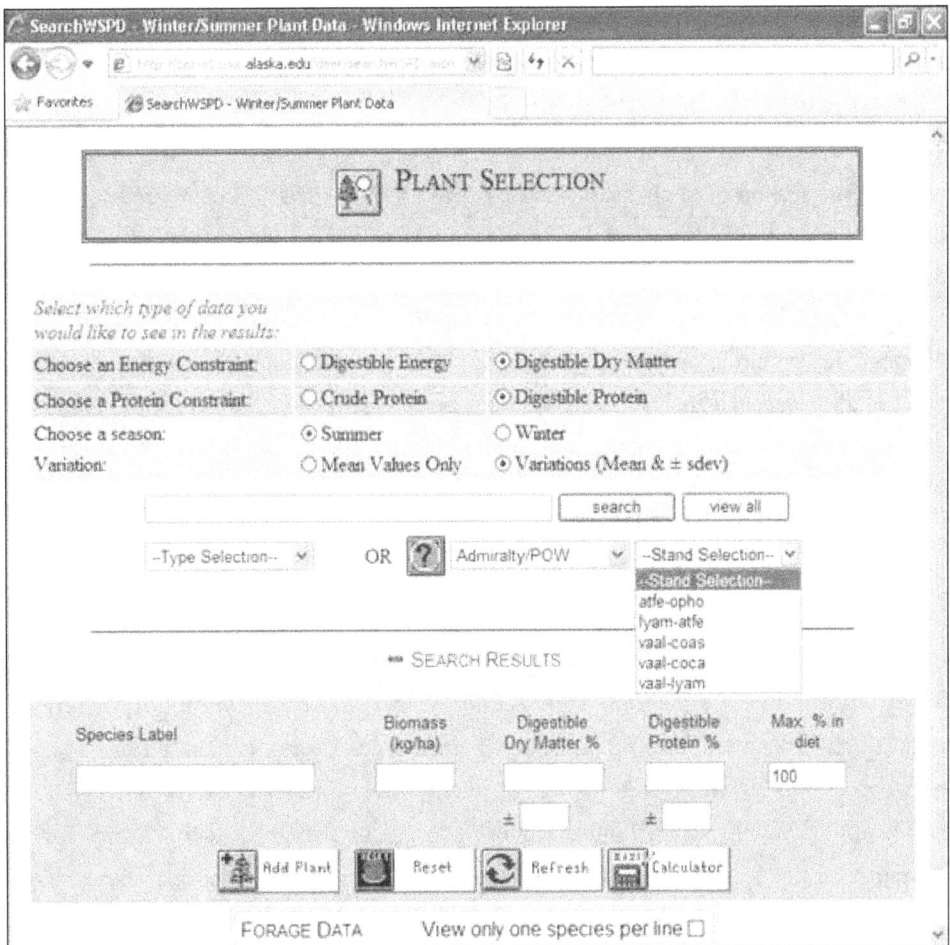

Figure 4—Screen print of Web page where plant biomass database is accessed through drop-down menus to the right of the question mark in the center of screen: first drop-down menu is "Region Selection" ("Admiralty/POW" has been selected); second is "Stand Selection."

southeastern Alaska. We intend to add to this database continuously as more biomass data become available. The user can access this database by hitting the "Search Database" button on the Deer Page Main Menu. The user then can select a "Region" (group of data, each group collected in one study) and then a "Stand" (one habitat description) within that region. Alternatively, the user can directly enter their own original data rather than use a data set from our database. Whenever "plant codes" (app. 3) are included to describe the forage, FRESH will link them to the same plant codes in our forage nutrition database to provide estimates of digestible energy and protein. If the user has their own nutritional data, then those data can be input directly instead of using our linked database. Our nutritional database is a compilation of nutritional data (app. 2) from southeastern Alaska. However, it currently is based on only five studies. More data are needed. We intend to add to this database periodically as additional data become available.

Access to the databases, entering or importing original data, and data requirements are outlined in the "Web-based Application User's Manual" accessed via the "User's Manuals" topic on the Deer tab of the Web site.

Energy and Protein Constraints

The user must specify the units of measurement for the energy and protein constraints, the season of analysis, and whether to include variation in the estimates of nutritional quality (see below). There are two options provided for each of the energy and protein constraints (fig. 4). For energy, there is either "Digestible Energy" or "Digestible Dry Matter." For protein, there is either "Crude Protein" or "Digestible Protein." We provide the choice because not all data in our database, and not all users' original data, are in the preferred currencies of digestible energy and digestible protein (see app. 1 for suggested field and laboratory methods for obtaining original data).

Although most "energy" values are expressed in terms of digestible dry matter, digestible energy is the preferred energy constraint. Digestible energy is the product of dry matter digestibility (percentage) and gross energy (kilojoules/gram [kJ/g] or kilocalories/gram [kcal/g]) of the forage. Of these two factors, dry matter digestibility is far more variable than is gross energy. Dry matter digestibility typically ranges between about 30 to 90 percent, whereas gross energy typically ranges between 17.6 to 20.1 kJ/g (4.2 to 4.8 kcal/g) with most forages close to 18.8 kJ/g (4.5 kcal/g) (Robbins 1993). Thus, studies of forage quality frequently emphasize measures of dry matter digestibility rather than taking on the additional expense of including gross energy. If one assumes a constant gross energy value of 18.8 kJ/g across all forages, then a "nutritional requirement" for dry matter digestibility can be calculated for any given daily digestible energy requirement and daily dry matter intake (see deer metabolic requirements, table 1).

The difference between energy units of kJ and kcal is simply a constant 1.0 kcal = 4.1868 kJ. Kilocalorie is an older preferred unit, while kJ is the currently preferred unit. Many older data sets are in units of kcal. Thus, we provide the option for either. However, if the user is using our linked nutritional database, then they will be limited to whatever units are in the database.

Similarly, digestible protein is the preferred measure of dietary protein content and nutritional constraint. However, measures of digestible protein are relatively few in the literature, whereas crude protein data (or total nitrogen [N]; crude protein = total N times 6.25) are common. We caution the user, however, that the

Table 1—Suggested input for deer nutritional constraints (for adult female Sitka black-tail in early July and mid winter) (dry-matter intake and requirements for metabolizable energy, digestible dry matter, and digestible protein)

Season and nutritional status	Metabolizable energy requirement	Dry-matter intake	Digestible dry matter	Digestible protein
	kcal/day	*g/day*	- - - - - *Percent* - - - - -	
Summer:				
Maintenance, no fawns	2,350	1,220	50	4.8
With single fawn	3,100	1,340	60	8.0
With twin fawns	3,500	1,470	62	10.0
Winter:				
From high-quality summer range	960	525	48	1.8
From low-quality summer range	1,050	525	52	1.8

Metabolizable energy (ME) **requirement** and **dry-matter intake** (DMI): Parker et al. 1999 (fig. 12 for ME and fig. 8 for DMI), assuming a summer body weight of 42 kg and winter body weight of 35 kg (Parker et al. 1999) and that voluntary DMI increases with increasing ME (within reasonable limits).

Minimum concentration of **digestible dry matter** (DDM) of diet, given the specified values of ME and DMI and an assumed gross energy content of 4.5 kcal/g and ME coefficient of 0.85 (Robbins 1993):
DDM = (ME ÷ 0.85 ÷ 4.5 ÷ DMI) × 100.

Minimum concentration of **digestible protein** (DP) of diet, given the specified value of DMI and assumed body weights (as above) is calculated as follows:
Dietary crude protein content (percentage) for maintenance = ([[EUN + MFN (DMI) × 6.25] ÷ DMI ÷ 0.74] × 100) (Robbins 1993: 183) where EUN (endogenous urinary nitrogen) and MFN (metabolic fecal nitrogen) are calculated as in Parker et al. (1999) with body weights (as above).

Dietary crude protein content (percentage) for lactation:
Peak protein requirement for a single fawn = 505 g/day of milk, with a protein content of 0.069 g/g and a digestibility coefficient of 0.95 (Sadleir 1980): 505 × 0.069 ÷ 0.95 = 36.68 g/day. Requirement for twin fawns is 1.67 times that of a single fawn (Robbins 1993: 213): 36.68 × 1.67 = 61.25 g/day.

Total requirement of dietary crude protein content = maintenance plus lactation.
Conversion of crude protein (CP) to digestible protein (DP) as follows (Hanley et al. 1992):
DP = -3.87 + 0.9283 (CP).

Sources: Hanley et al. 1992, Parker et al. 1999, Robins 1993, Sadleir 1980.

differences between digestible protein and crude protein can be very significant biologically—usually far more so than differences between digestible energy and digestible dry matter.

Other Foraging Constraints, Optional

Two additional foraging constraints are included for "advanced" users (we recommend not using them for initial analyses): (1) the maximum percentage that any one species can contribute to the total biomass of the solution set ("diet"), and (2) the minimum amount of total biomass acceptable for a solution.

The first is somewhat similar to the forage-specific upper limit (maximum constraint) that the user can specify for each forage (see "Factors Affecting Nutrition and Palatability" in general discussion of FRESH), except that this time, the constraint is not forage-specific; it applies for **any** (unspecified) forage that approaches the value of the constraint in the linear program solution. The reasoning behind this constraint is that deer are generalist herbivores and require a floristically diverse diet. Most of their forages contain noxious compounds, which are not a problem when consumed in moderation, but can be toxic when consumed in excess. Thus, no one or few forages can completely dominate a diet to the exclusion of others. For example, skunk cabbage (*Lysichiton americanus* Hulten & H. St. John) is a very good forage with high values of digestible energy and digestible protein in summer, but it also contains oxalic acid crystals, cyanide compounds, and excessive concentration of water. Skunk cabbage often occurs in extensive patches, dominating the vegetation of some habitats. However, it could not constitute such a predominant proportion of the total diet of deer. The user might want to guard against such occurrence by specifying a generic (not forage-specific) constraint on the maximum amount that any one forage (like skunk cabbage, or others not anticipated beforehand) can contribute to the final solution. We recommend that this constraint not be used at the stand level of application, however, because deer have access to other forage resources well beyond the stand itself. It can be useful at the landscape level of application because that is the scale at which individual deer can select their diets (the user specifies the home range size in the landscape level, GIS application). A generic constraint of 40 percent might be a reasonable upper limit in that case. However, this constraint seems most useful in subsequent gaming or exploratory analyses rather than initial analysis. The default value of this constraint is 100 percent (i.e., no effect).

The "minimum amount of biomass" constraint is a simplifying consideration that there exists a lower limit of total forage biomass beyond which a deer cannot forage profitably (in a time-effective manner) in a habitat. Studies of dry matter intake as a function of available forage biomass (the so-called "functional response") indicate an asymptotic, threshold response that varies with animal body size (Spalinger and Hobbs 1992, Wickstrom et al. 1984). For a deer the size of a female Sitka black-tail, the threshold is low, about 25 kg/ha (Spalinger et al. 1988, Wickstrom et al. 1984). Thus, only in habitats with very sparse forage does the quantity of forage, per se, interfere with the foraging process. This constraint enables the user to take foraging efficiency into account by discounting the value of very sparse habitat accordingly. The way the constraint works is that whatever value is specified by the user is subtracted from the total usable forage of the solution set before that value is divided by the daily dry-matter intake of a deer. For example, if 25 kg/ha is specified as "minimum amount of total biomass," and the linear program yielded a solution of 100 kg/ha "total biomass used," then the 25 kg/ha would be subtracted from the 100 kg/ha before dividing into the daily dry-matter intake per deer (yielding deer days per hectare). Obviously, the effect of this "constraint" (note that it is not a constraint in the linear program itself) is much more pronounced in forage-sparse than forage-abundant habitats. Unlike the "maximum percentage of diet" constraint (above), this minimum biomass constraint is more appropriately applied at the stand level of application than at the landscape level of application, because it becomes increasingly problematic with increasing patchiness of vegetation. (An implicit assumption of this constraint is that the forage is evenly distributed in the habitat, i.e., not patchy.) In practice, we've found that this constraint tends to mask interesting output for low-biomass stands, and therefore, we recommend against its use in initial analysis. Its default value is 0 kg/ha (i.e., no effect).

Importance of Variation in Nutritional Values and Habitat Biomass Values

Nutritional values—

The user may choose to include variation in the estimates of nutritional quality (mean + standard deviation) when doing the calculations or simply work with mean values (only) for each forage. We highly recommend including variation. The standard deviations in our database simply reflect the variation in values reported from various studies. However, it is important to recognize that nutritional quality of any given forage at any given time can be variable, from site to site, within the same site, and even within different leaves or twigs of the same plant, depending on site, microenvironment, phenological differences, and within-plant resource allocation. Thus, the nutritional values of forages in our database are just best approximations, not precise, fixed values. Including variation in the analysis provides consideration that the nutritional values are not precise and fixed.

The user may choose to include variation in the estimates of nutritional quality (mean + standard deviation) when doing the calculations or simply work with mean values (only) for each forage. We highly recommend including variation.

The way FRESH deals with nutritional variation is as follows: The available biomass of each forage is divided into three equal groups of biomass, differing in their nutritional values, and each group is then treated as a separate, unique forage in the analysis. The nutritional values assigned to the three groups are (1) the mean plus one standard deviation, (2) the mean, and (3) the mean minus one standard deviation. Both energy and protein values are raised (and lowered) together, because digestible energy and digestible protein tend to be correlated within the same forage (Hanley and McKendrick 1983, Johnstone et al. 2002, Leslie et al. 1984). Approximately 68 percent of the time, the values of a normally distributed random variable will fall within one standard deviation of the mean (i.e., 16 percent on either tail of the distribution) (Snedecor and Cochran 1967). Thus, our three biomass groups for each forage would be of approximately equal size if the data were distributed normally (strictly, the groups would include 32 percent on either end and 36 percent in the middle).

When the user includes nutritional variation in the analysis, the forage list becomes very large (three times the number of forages). The output from that analysis may be important to the user, to see exactly which of the expanded forages were included in the solution. However, we also provide the user an option of viewing the analysis and results with only one line per forage (rather than three lines). Most users probably will prefer to view only one line per forage, whereas the analysis works on all three "lines" (biomass groups). See the Web-based User's Manual (accessed on Web site) for details.

Nutritional variation is important in application of the analysis because the nutritional constraints in the linear programming model are precise. Thus, most forages tend to be either included or excluded in the solution, with very few partial inclusions. When nutritional variation is included in the analysis, partial inclusion of forages is common and much more reflective of the variability that exists in nature.

Habitat biomass values—

A similar problem to that of nutritional variation is that estimates of biomass within a habitat also are not highly precise, fixed values. There is always variation among samples even within the same stand; greater precision can be obtained with greater sampling intensity in the field. However, that is probably a lesser problem in comparison to variation between stands of the same "habitat type" (a type within a classification of types).

The FRESH system does not currently deal explicitly with either kind of variation in habitat biomass values. However, the user can use FRESH to analyze both types of variation. For within-stand variation, we recommend a "running-means" analysis, where the Deer Days/Ha value (output solution) is plotted against an increasing sample size (e.g., number of sample quadrats) within the stand, and the variation in that value is seen graphically. For example, if the stand's vegetation had been sampled with 30 quadrats (e.g., a 0.5- or 1.0-m^2 sampling frame), then the mean biomass of each forage in the stand could be calculated for various combinations of the 30 quadrats (e.g., for the first 10 only, then for the first 15, then 20, etc., or any other combination). The user might proceed by calculating five (for example) descriptions of the stand, each time using an increasing number of quadrats until finally using all quadrats for the last description. The FRESH analysis could then be applied to each of the five descriptions (arrays of available forages), yielding a Deer Days/Ha value for each. A graphical plot of the Deer Days/Ha values against the increasing number of quadrats would provide a graphical analysis of the effect of increasing sample size (quadrats) on the precision of the Deer Days/Ha estimate for that stand. This provides **one** metric of variation within that stand, rather than n independent metrics, where n is the number of forages in the stand. And, this one metric of variation (in Deer Days/Ha) is precisely the metric of greatest interest in terms of overall habitat value to deer. Alternatively, various statistical subsampling techniques could be used to estimate the within-stand variation similarly.

For variation among stands of the same habitat type, we simply recommend that the FRESH analysis be applied to each stand, separately, yielding a Deer Days/Ha value for each stand. The mean Deer Days/Ha value for the habitat type then can be calculated as the mean (and variation) of the Deer Days/Ha values across all stands within that habitat type. Not only will that approach yield an estimate of among-stand variation in addition to the mean, but the mean Deer Days/Ha value will likely differ from that of one analysis applied to a composite food array calculated across all stands. The mean of the individual stand values is the true mean, because the value from the composite array is based on a much more diverse vegetation than actually occurred in any one stand.

▢▢ ▢ ▢▢▢▢ ▢ ▢▢▢▢▢▢ ▢▢▢▢▢▢▢▢▢▢▢

The FRESH system can convert any summer habitat description (list of forages and their biomass) to an estimated description of forage availability in winter through a relatively simple process (box 5). It requires that the user specify the following attributes for each forage: (1) "percentage in winter," and the forage's height profile in terms of (2) minimum and (3) maximum height in centimeters.

"Percentage in winter" is the snow-free availability of the forage in winter expressed as a percentage of its availability in summer. "Percentage in winter" of most forages is usually either 0 percent (deciduous) or 100 percent (evergreen). For example, leaves of deciduous shrubs and herbs are 0 percent, whereas twigs of most shrubs are 100 percent; leaves of evergreen species are 100 percent. Some species,

Box 5: Converting a Summer Biomass Data Set (array) to Winter Biomass Availability

Steps:

1. Additional data requirements for each forage (to be entered into the summer data set):
   a. "Proportion of Summer Biomass" (e.g., deciduous forages = 0; evergreen forages are >0 but may be <1.0)
   b. Minimum height aboveground (cm)
   c. Maximum height aboveground (cm)
   d. Winter (1 Feb.) nutritional values (e.g., dry matter digestibility or digestible energy, and digestible protein).

2. Multiply summer biomass value by its "Proportion of Summer Biomass" factor for each species. This provides each forage's "Snow-free Winter Biomass" (B_{sf}).

3. Determine height profile (minimum to maximum heights) for each forage and assume that the forage's biomass is distributed uniformly throughout its height profile.

4. Determine snow depth in the stand on 1 February (see "Snow Depth Equations" and box 6). Snow depth is a function of the stand's elevation, aspect, slope, and overstory canopy coverage.

5. Reduce each forage's biomass in proportion to its height profile that is "buried" in snow. Use the following equation, where "D_{asc}" is the snow depth in the stand, "Min" is the forage's minimum height, "Max" is the forage's maximum height, "B_{sf}" is the forage's snow-free winter biomass, and "B_s" is the forage's biomass adjusted for burial by snow, assuming a simple linear bottom-up burial process:

$$B_s = B_{sf} \times (1 - [D_{asc} - Min]/[Max - Min]),$$

where the maximum value of $[D_{asc} - Min]/[Max - Min]$ cannot exceed 1.0

For blueberry shrubs (*Vaccinium ovalifolium, V. parvifolium, V. alaskaense*) and salal (*Gaultheria shallon*), B_s is further reduced to incorporate a nonlinear logarithmic decay rate between snow depths of 20 cm (no nonlinear effect) and 100 cm (complete burial) for blueberry, and between 1 cm (no nonlinear effect) and 50 cm (complete burial) for salal:

For blueberry at snow depths between 20 and 100 cm:

$B_s = B_{s20} (Y /100)$, where B_{s20} is the snow-free value of B_s at 20-cm depth and Y is the percentage remaining at greater depths.

$Y = 286.14 - 62.13 (\ln X)$, where X is the snow depth in centimeters.

$$B_s = 0 \text{ for all depths } >100 \text{ cm.}$$

For salal at snow depths between 1 and 50 cm:

$B_s = B_{s01} (Y / 100)$, where B_{s01} is the snow-free value of B_s at 1-cm depth and Y is the percentage remaining at greater depths.

$Y = 100.00 - 25.58 (\ln X)$, where X is the snow depth in centimeters.

$$B_s = 0 \text{ for all depths } > 50 \text{ cm.}$$

Running the model for winter:

6. Use the B_s value and the winter nutritional values for each forage; change the model's user-specified metabolic requirements and dry-matter intake values to appropriate winter values; and run the model.

however, are partially available in winter. For example, the fern *Dryopteris dilatata* is deciduous, but it overwinters as a fiddlehead at ground surface in the forest floor and is eaten by deer when the ground surface is not frozen (Gillingham et al. 2000). Thus, its "percentage in winter" is less than 100 percent, but greater than 0 percent. The height profile of each forage (minimum and maximum heights above the ground surface) provides a description of the vertical zone in which the forage biomass occurs during snow-free winter conditions.

Given the above information about each forage, FRESH converts its summer biomass to winter biomass availability through the following steps. First, the summer biomass is multiplied by its proportional availability in winter ("percentage in winter"). This provides a winter estimate under snow-free conditions. When snow is present (see "Snow Submodel," below), the availability of the snow-free biomass is further reduced by burial in snow, with two simplifying assumptions: (1) that the forage biomass is evenly distributed throughout the height profile of the forage, and (2) that burial by snow occurs as a bottom-up process (i.e., forage below the snow depth is not available, whereas forage above the snow depth is available). There is no accounting for stem bending or entrapment in the snowpack, with two exceptions: blueberry shrubs (*Vaccinium ovalifolium*, *V. parvifolium*, and *V. alaskaense*) and salal (*Gaultheria shallon*). Blueberry and salal are important winter forages throughout the range of Sitka black-tails and northern range of Columbian black-tails (*O. h. columbianus*). Blueberry species are important because their twigs are relatively nutritious, and salal because its leaves are evergreen. The snow burial process has been studied for both blueberry and salal, and stem bending and entrapment in the snowpack has been found to be important in both, resulting in nonlinear decay rates in their availability with increasing depth of snow (Hovey 1987, Hovey and Harestad 1992, Jenkins et al. 1990, Vales 1986, White et al. 2009). We have incorporated that effect for blueberry twigs and salal by assuming that blueberry is unaffected by entrapment in the snowpack at snow depths of 20 cm or less but is entrapped at >20 cm, so its availability decreases in a nonlinear, logarithmic fashion between 20 and 100 cm with all twigs buried by snow at 100-cm depth and greater, regardless of how tall the blueberry is in snow-free conditions. We have assumed a similar process for the lower growing, leafy salal at snow depths from 1 to 50 cm, with complete burial at all depths of 50 cm and greater (see box 5 for details).

Both blueberry and salal have relatively limber stems and are especially susceptible to bending and entrapment in the snowpack. Other species of shrubs have not been studied, so we have incorporated the nonlinear burial process only for blueberry and salal; other browse species follow the simple, linear, bottom-up burial process.

In addition, the user also must change the animal constraints (metabolic requirements, table 1) to appropriate values for winter and provide values of nutritional quality for each forage in winter. The FRESH nutritional database includes winter nutritional values for users who do not have their own and substitutes them in place of summer nutritional values for forages that are in the database.

Although it is a very simple procedure to convert a summer habitat description to a winter habitat description (one keystroke in the FRESH system—see the Web-based User's Manual accessed via the Web site), it is not possible to convert a winter description to a summer description. The missing (deciduous) forages would be unknown.

Snow Submodel

The current snow submodel is best considered a prototype or first approximation model. It is based on very few data and needs to be field verified and, quite possibly, adjusted. The data consist of a 33-year record (fig. 5) from USDA NRCS snow courses accessed from the Eaglecrest Road near Juneau (USDA NRCS Web site: http://www.ak.nrcs.usda.gov/Snow/southeast.html) and corresponding snow depth measurements taken by the National Oceanic and Atmospheric Administration National Climate Data Center station at the Juneau International Airport (USDC Web site: http://hurricane.ncdc.noaa.gov/dly/DLY), all for 1 February, 1977 to 2009, and a published regression relationship (Hanley and Rose 1987) between overstory

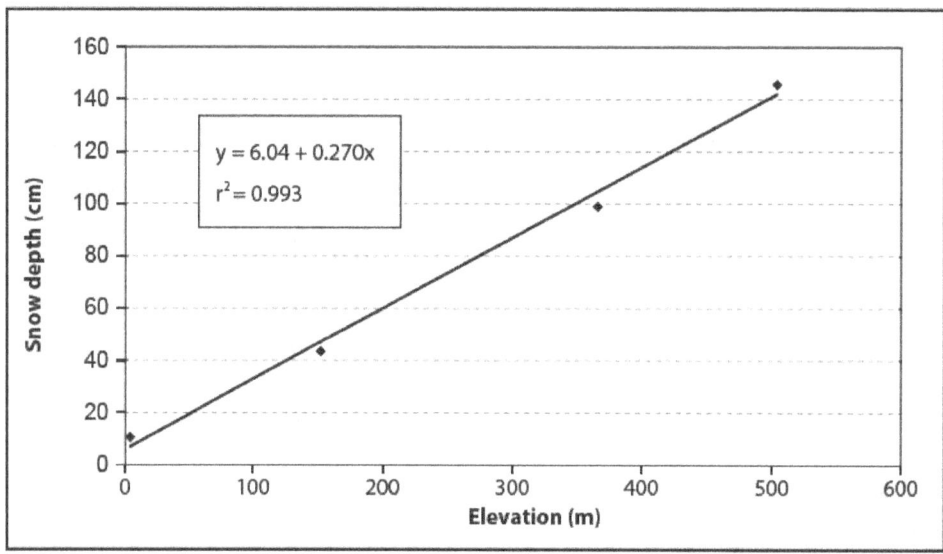

Figure 5—1 February snow depth, mean of 1977–2009 observations (33 years) from USDA Natural Resources and Conservation Service (USDA NRCS) snow courses on Eaglecrest Road and Eaglecrest (elevations 152, 366, and 503 m) and from National Oceanographic and Atmospheric Administration National Climate Data Center data at Juneau International Airport (elevation 4 m), Juneau, Alaska.

canopy coverage and its effect on snow depth (fig. 6). The Eaglecrest Road and airport sites are all in close proximity, differing mainly in elevation (5 to 503 m), thus providing the best available long-term data set for an elevation gradient in southeastern Alaska.

The date of 1 February was chosen as representative of mid-winter snow conditions. It provides a winter index for the snapshot analysis from FRESH. Users should keep in mind that winter snowpacks vary continuously throughout the winter, and that the FRESH analysis is a snapshot at one point in time, not an average for the whole winter.

The snow submodel (see box 6) predicts the depth of a snowpack under the forest canopy as a function of elevation, slope, aspect, overstory canopy coverage of the stand, and depth of snow in a level, open area at sea level. The snow depth at sea level is specified by the user and provides a means of increasing or decreasing the snowpack in relation to more or less snow as a function of weather, time of winter, or geographic climate zone (e.g., outer coast versus mainland sites, northern versus southern sites). It allows the user to explore how habitat quality changes with greater or lesser amounts of snow at a given base area (sea level). The specified

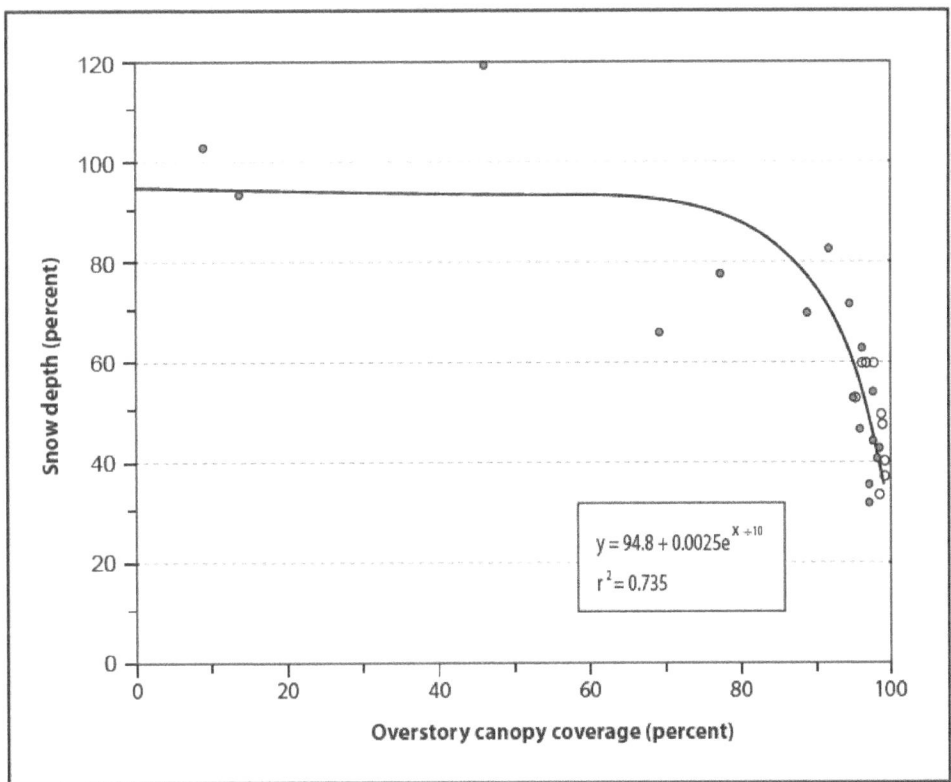

Figure 6—Mean snow depth in the forest (as a percentage of depth in the open) as a function of overstory canopy coverage. Each point is the mean of five sampling periods. Solid circles represent uneven-aged stands; open circles represent even-aged stands. (From Hanley and Rose 1987.)

Box 6: Snow Submodel Calculations

Units of measurement:

   Snow depth (centimeters)

   Elevation (meters)

   Aspect (degrees, 0 and 360 = true north)

   Slope (degrees)

   Overstory canopy coverage (percent)

   Plant heights (centimeters)

Snow-depth equations:

   Snow depth (D) in a level, open area as a function of elevation (E)

   $$D = 10.3 + 0.27(E)$$

   D is in centimeters; E is in meters.

   It is always the starting point.

Effect of aspect (A), in relation to slope (S), on snow depth (D_a)

   $$D_a = D + 0.33(\cos A)(\tan S) \times D$$

   D_a is in centimeters and is a non-negative value. The least it can be is zero. 0.33(cos A)(tan S) × D simply modifies the elevation value, but it interacts with slope. The maximum value that tan(S) is allowed to take is 1.00, which occurs at a slope of 45 degrees (100 percent). Slopes greater than 45 degrees are treated the same as 45 degrees. The 0.33 constant is strictly arbitrary, yielding a 100 percent greater depth on due-North than due-South aspects on 45° slopes, and a 27 percent greater depth on 20° slopes.

Effect of slope (S) on snow depth (D_s)

   $$D_s = D \times \cos(S)$$

   cos(S) is a proportional multiplier ranging between 0.0 and 1.0.

   This effect of slope is independent of aspect. It is the gravitational effect (snow moving downhill) and the sublimation effect (exposure to air; greater surface area with greater slope).

Effect of overstory canopy coverage (C) on snow depth (D_c)

   $$D_c = D \times (100 - 0.0025e^{C/10})/100$$

   This equation is from Hanley and Rose (1987), with modification. The parenthetical expression is a percentage multiplier. Note, however, that canopy coverage was measured with a spherical densiometer.

Combined snow depth model (D_{sac})

   $$D_{sac} = [D + 0.33(\cos A)(\tan S) \times D] \times \cos(S) \times (100 - 0.0025e^{C/10})/100 ,$$

   where D is always an elevation-dependent starting point.

(continued on next page)

Thus, for example: a stand at 300 m elevation, 180° aspect (due south), 25° slope (= 56 percent), and 90 percent overstory canopy coverage would have a predicted snow depth of 55.8 cm (i.e., 61 percent of D for a level, open-canopied area at 300 m elevation). Individually, the factors would have the following effects:

$$D = 10.3 + 0.27(E) = 91.3 \text{ cm}$$
$$D_a = 91.3 + 0.33(\cos 180)(\tan 25) \times 91.3 = 77.3 \text{ cm}$$
$$D_s = 91.3 \times \cos(25) = 82.7 \text{ cm}$$
$$D_c = 91.3 \times (100 - 0.0025e^{90/10})/100 = 72.8 \text{ cm}$$

Obviously, the effect of elevation is overwhelming. That is why it is always the starting point.

depth at sea level thus provides a standard for comparison of any stands differing in their topographic settings or overstory canopy coverage.

The calculations (box 6) involve the following relations: (1) The effect of elevation is predicted by a data-based regression relationship (fig. 5) between elevation and depth by using the regression slope and the user-specified sea-level depth as the Y-intercept (note that with a negative Y-intercept value [<0 cm], the "snow line" [snow depth >0 cm] moves up the mountains in elevation). The elevation-predicted depth is then modified by (2) effect of slope (a cosine function where 0 slope has no effect, and all the snow slides off at 90 degrees slope), (3) effect of aspect interacting with slope (a cosine function interacting with a tangent function, where snow depth is increased on northerly aspects and decreased on southerly aspects), and (4) effect of overstory canopy coverage (an exponentially decreasing function with increasing canopy coverage, fig. 6). Although overstory mass (e.g., wood volume) also may influence snow interception (Kirchhoff and Schoen 1987), best predictive models across wide ranges of young-growth and old-growth stands have been obtained with canopy coverage (Hanley and Rose 1987, Harestad and Bunnell 1981).

An optional, habitat-specific factor, called the "Shrub/Slash-Interaction Multiplier," is provided to allow the user to account for the effect of dense shrubs and logging or thinning slash in holding snow above the ground, thereby increasing the effective depth of snow in that particular habitat. Dense shrubs in high-biomass, young clearcuts, for example, intercept much snow and hold it above ground level, having the snow-burial effect of much deeper snow. The Shrub/Slash-Interaction Multiplier is a user-specified constant that simply multiplies the calculated snow depth of the given habitat (as described above and in box 6) by the constant. Its default value is 1.0 (i.e., no effect).

The effect of snow depth in FRESH-Deer is on forage availability only, through burial (see "Summer to Winter Conversion" above). We have not attempted to model energy costs of locomotion through snow, because the effect of snowpack on mobility of deer in southeastern Alaska is highly variable. Frozen crusts on the snow surface, resulting from wet snow freezing, are common in this region, and deer can easily walk on frozen crusts without breaking through (Parker et al. 1999). When snow is not crusted (e.g., very fresh or falling), then deer may sink in it and experience high costs of locomotion (Parker et al. 1984). Overall, however, energy costs for locomotion in snow are a relatively minor variable in the winter energy budget of black-tailed deer in southeastern Alaska, especially in comparison with basal metabolic energy costs and the snowpack's effects of reduced energy intake (forage quality, especially) (Hanley and McKendrick 1985, Parker et al. 1999). Similarly, energy costs for thermoregulation are unimportant for black-tailed deer in southeastern Alaska in virtually all but the most open, exposed habitats (Parker 1988, Parker and Gillingham 1990, Parker and Robbins 1984, Parker et al. 1999).

Interpretation of Output

The output provides the total number of Deer Days/Ha the habitat can support plus the following key information (cross-referenced to fig. 7): A listing of all key data used in the analysis—(1) the animal constraints specified by the user (i.e., metabolic requirements; immediately below the yellow bar labeled "Animal Constraints"); (2) the total biomass of forage available in the habitat (second line from top, 269.8500); (3) the complete list of forages (data summary box immediately beneath "Plant Data and Amount Used"), their biomass, nutritional values, and forage-specific dietary constraints ("Maximum percentage in diet"). And it provides key results from the analysis—(4) the total suitable biomass used in the solution (third line from top, 129.8168); (5) its mean nutritional qualities (fourth and fifth lines from top, 60.000 and 8.410; (6) the biomass used of each forage (the amount that each forage contributes to the solution; third column from right in data summary box); (7) the amount used expressed as a percentage of that forage's availability in the habitat (second column from right in same summary box); and (8) the amount used expressed as a percentage of the total suitable biomass used in the solution (furthest right column in same summary box).

Comparison of the total biomass available and the total biomass used in the solution tells whether total biomass of forage was the limiting factor (all available biomass would have been used) or nutritional/dietary constraints were limiting ("Total Biomass Used" would be less than "Total Available Biomass"). Comparisons of the mean nutritional composition (e.g., mean digestible energy or dry matter: mean digestible protein) of the solution set ("Total Biomass Used") with the user-specified animal constraints identify the limiting constraint(s). For example, if the mean concentration of digestible energy in the solution equals the digestible energy constraint, while the mean concentration of digestible protein in the solution exceeds the digestible protein constraint, then digestible energy was the limiting factor, and digestible protein was not limiting. The "Percent Used" value for each forage provides a measure of that forage's relative value in the solution set, and therefore, relative value to deer. Forages that were 100 percent used (included in the solution) were highly valuable forages: forages that were 0 percent used (not included in the solution) contributed nothing and may as well not have been there: forages used between 0 and 100 percent were of intermediate value. The relative contribution of each forage to the total solution (the "Percent of Total" column) provides a description of the solution "diet." It reflects the combined effects of the

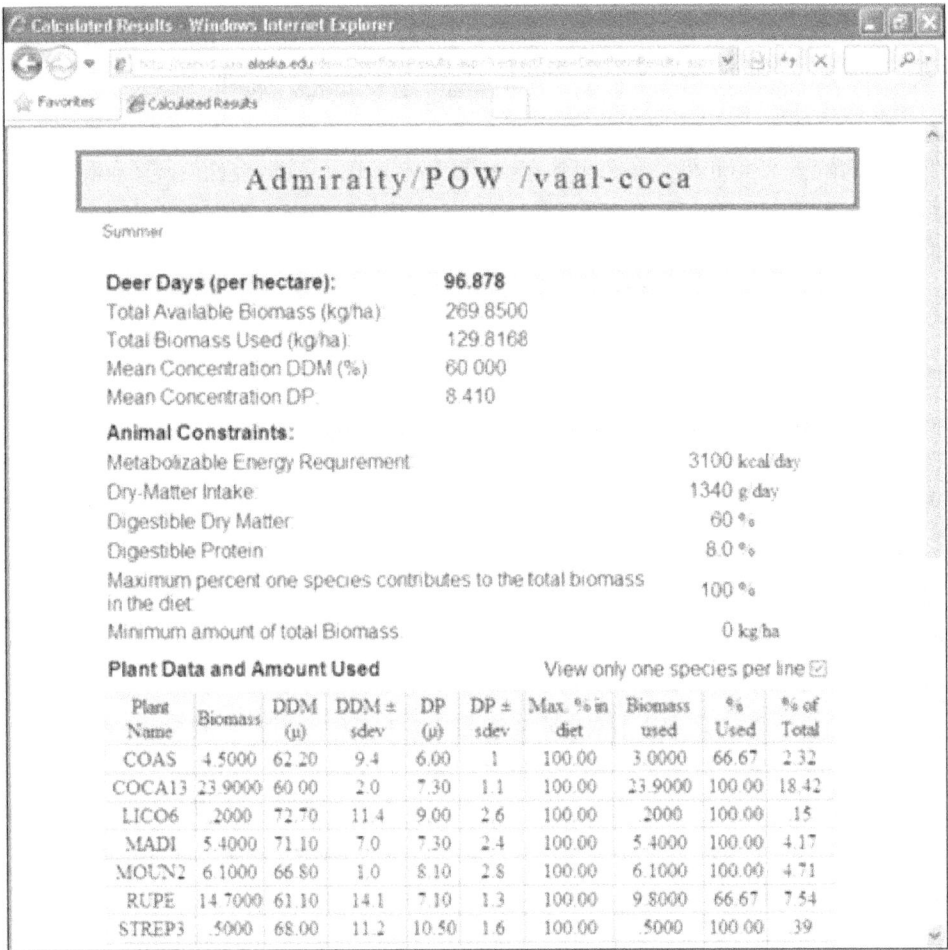

Figure 7—Screen print of the solution to a habitat from the biomass database in summer for a doe with one fawn. The full Web page includes the results for all 30 forages (only the first seven are seen here).

relative quality of each forage and its absolute biomass availability. Comparison of the "Percent of Total" with the "Maximum Percentage in Diet" constraint for any forage tells whether the forage's contribution to the solution was limited because of its abundance (available biomass), nutritional quality (either digestible energy or digestible protein or both), or the forage-specific "Maximum Percentage in Diet" constraint. Note that these values for any given forage will differ from habitat to habitat because of relative differences in forage availabilities.

All of those comparisons provide important insight into understanding the Deer Days/Ha solution and the food and nutritional limitations of the habitat. For additional insight, the user might want to game the system by editing values of available biomass or nutritional quality of select forages and repeating the analysis, or by varying nutritional constraints (or snow depth in winter) and repeating the analysis. This begets a sensitivity analysis, which helps evaluate the relative roles and effects of various factors in any given habitat-environment situation.

□□□ □ □□□□□

The GIS Application for landscape-level analyses requires that the user specify a "grid area" ("pixels per grid"), or window size, for the moving-windows analysis (fig. 8). Forage resources from all habitats falling within each "grid" or "window" are combined into one array of forage resources for that grid. The grid size specified by the user should reflect the scale of habitat use by an individual animal, i.e., a typical home range size. Mean home range size for Sitka black-tailed deer has been reported to range from about 80 ha (200 ac) (Admiralty Island—Schoen and Kirchhoff 1985) to 200 ha (500 ac) (Prince of Wales Island—Yeo and Peek 1992) with seasonal differences in "core areas" (zones of high use) for winter being about 70 percent the size of those for summer (32 ha winter vs. 45 ha summer, Prince of Wales Island).

Users must choose a home range size for their analysis and divide it into the size of a pixel in their GIS system to determine the number of pixels for a sampling grid. The sampling grid in the FRESH system is square; thus the grid size specification should be the square root of the number of pixels the user wants per grid. For example, for a 100-ha home range size and a pixel size of 30 × 30 m (900 m^2), the user-specified grid size would be 33 (i.e., square root of [100 × 10,000 / 900] = 33.3).

Given the variation reported for home range sizes of Sitka black-tails, users might want to try several runs with FRESH, varying the grid size specification for each run, to examine sensitivity to home range assumptions in the analysis of their study area. Sensitivity to home range size will vary with habitats and their spatial pattern uniquely for any given landscape.

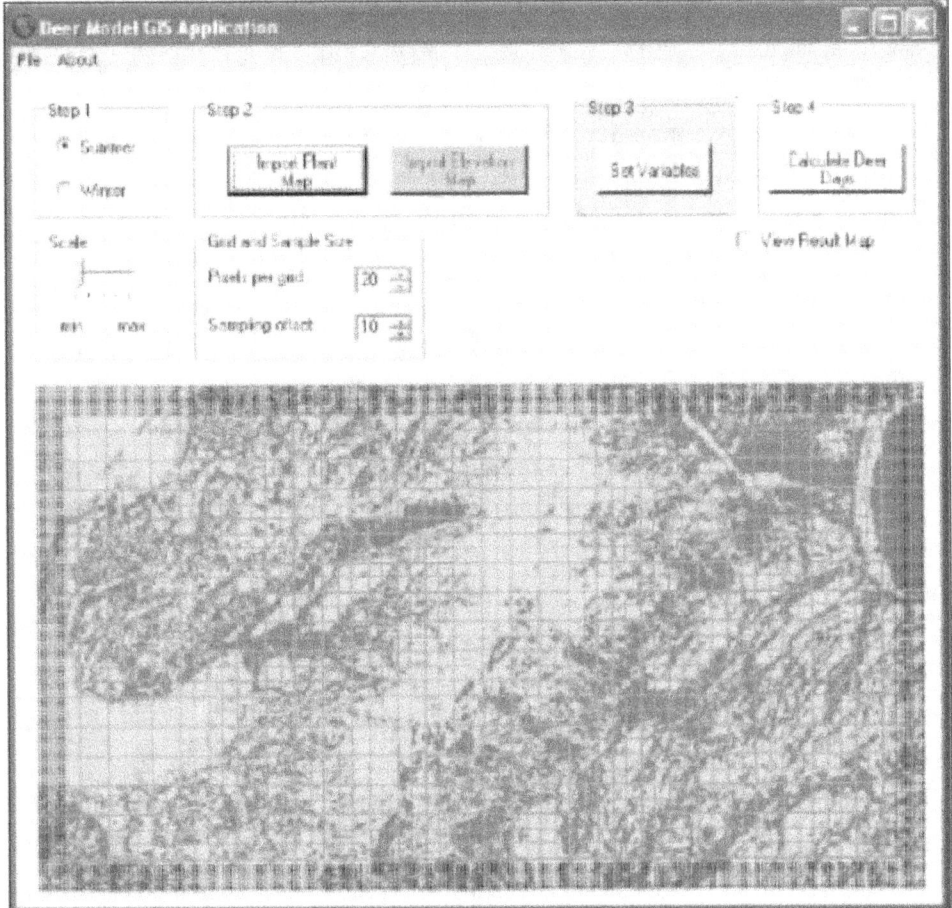

Figure 8—Screen print of the geographic information system application showing the sampling grid and how grid size (pixels per grid) and sampling offset are user-specified.

User's Manuals

User's manuals are available directly from the Web site by clicking on the "User's Manuals" heading under the Deer tab. Users should begin with the Web-based Application User's Manual to understand how the system works and its data requirements. For large-scale, spatial analysis, the user will need to use the GIS-based application, which is accessed through the "Export Data" button on the Deer main page. The GIS Application Instruction Manual is available there, as well as in the User's Manuals section.

Management Implications

The most valuable aspects of FRESH may not be the habitat values it provides, but rather the informative or educational value and systematic organization of habitat relations and data. FRESH-Deer, for example, not only calculates a quantitative value of habitat (Deer Days/Ha), but also identifies which forages are most important in providing that value, which nutritional constraints are most limiting, and how those relations change with seasonality, metabolic requirements, and snow depths. By varying individual factors, one at a time, users can see their relative importance and how their values affect the broader question of habitat value. Outcomes will differ with particular circumstances of the habitat patch or landscape. Such sensitivity analysis and gaming can yield much insight into "system behavior" of the deer-habitat interaction, at least in the way in which it has been modeled. Moreover, the modeling itself provides an explicit and entirely data-driven system of cause-and-effect relations determining habitat value for deer within habitat patches and landscapes. The model identifies key data needs (e.g., biomass and nutritional values of forages by habitat and silviculture treatment), future research needs (e.g., topography-overstory-snow relations), and ways of incorporating new understanding into a broader assessment of habitat quality for deer (e.g., adding deer habitat-selection behavior to the current food-based evaluation by incorporating a meta-analysis of resource utilization functions). It can, therefore, provide guidance in identifying priority research needs and be modified to incorporate new knowledge. The FRESH system is best thought of as a continuously evolving tool for organizing our understanding of deer-habitat relations and using that knowledge to evaluate habitat.

> **The FRESH system is best thought of as a continuously evolving tool for organizing our understanding of deer-habitat relations and using that knowledge to evaluate habitat.**

Immediate practical uses of FRESH-Deer are in evaluating the quality of individual patches of habitat (Web-based application) and their landscape pattern (GIS-based application). These are best considered as relative comparisons (i.e., relative value of one habitat or landscape pattern versus another), because the Deer Days/Ha values are, after all, indices of habitat value calculated for the particular time (e.g., early July or early February) and scenario (metabolic requirements, snow depth). To date, the stand-level analysis has been useful in evaluating differences in silviculture treatments (Cole et al. 2010, Zaborske et al. 2002) and forest composition (Hanley et al. 2006). The stand-level analysis currently provides the deer habitat analysis of the Tongass-Wide Young-Growth Studies (McClellan and DeSanto, in press), which form the basis of the young-growth monitoring program for the Tongass National Forest in Alaska. Work is currently underway to use the GIS application for timber planning analysis and young-growth silviculture planning by the Tongass National Forest and private lands owned and managed by the Sealaska Corporation. Landscape analyses will primarily be used for comparing various alternative planning scenarios and optimizing multiple resource objectives.

The FRESH-Deer system also provides the ability to compare the relative values of summer range and winter range for any given habitat or landscape. This has important implications for identifying the overall seasonal "bottleneck" of a given deer range, and it should be an important part of any habitat evaluation. In southeastern Alaska, deer-habitat concerns have frequently focused on "critical winter range," which was the sole focus of earlier unpublished deer-habitat models based on professional judgment. That was because winter is the time of greatest mortality of Sitka black-tailed deer, and winter survival was the focus of some of the earliest studies for deer management (Klein and Olson 1960, Olson 1952, Olson and Klein 1959), even though it was also known at that time that summer range is most important for growth and production of deer bodies and herds (Klein 1964, 1965). In fact, summer range is essential for black-tailed deer to recover body condition from winter, produce young, and build body reserves (fat, muscle) that enable them to survive the forage-poor conditions of winter (Parker et al. 1993, 1999). Thus, a focus on winter range alone is not only overly simplistic, it could be misleading and, especially, inadequate for guiding land management concerned with a landscape's capacity to produce and sustain deer. When evaluating a given landscape with FRESH-Deer, the user should evaluate that landscape for scenarios of both winter and summer. If the overall value of the landscape (its mean Deer Days/Ha value for all GIS pixels) is much lower in one season than the other, then management efforts directed at the lower capacity season will yield the greatest benefits for deer. When the relative seasonal values are nearly the same, then management treatments benefiting only one season without the other will be relatively limited in their potential effect.

FRESH-Deer also can provide an analytical basis for evaluating the consequences of new or even hypothetical changes in habitat for deer. For example, there is much interest today in global climate change and its possible effects on local environments and habitats. Consequences of climate change for deer would be manifested through changes in weather patterns (winter snowpack especially important for Sitka black-tails) and vegetation (species composition, production, maybe nutritional quality, landscape distribution of species and habitats). Analysis of the effects of climate change on deer habitat, therefore, should be directed at the presumed consequences for vegetation and snowpack, and those effects can be analyzed, in turn, with FRESH-Deer. Similarly, other community-wide or ecosystem-level changes, such as terrestrial effects of "marine-derived nutrients" from Pacific salmon (*Oncorhynchus* spp.) in riparian forests could be evaluated for deer on the basis of their effects on forage quality and quantity.

One important feature of black-tailed deer habitat in southeastern Alaska that is difficult to evaluate with FRESH-Deer is the role of gradients in snowmelt for the quality of summer range. Elevation gradients prolong the period of snowmelt through the summer, thereby extending the otherwise brief period of phenologically young, highly nutritious forage that becomes available shortly after vegetation emerges from a snowpack (Klein 1965). Similarly, topographically complex alpine and subalpine habitats do the same but on a smaller scale. The timing of spring and the availability of skunk cabbage (*Lysichiton americanus*) can be another important aspect of habitat for deer (Parker et al. 1999). Such temporal and spatial patterns can be analyzed with FRESH-Deer, but doing so requires considerably more analyses than simply one for early July (for example). For elevation gradients and seasonal timing, the landscape would need to be analyzed at several times during the growing season; for complex spatial gradients, the habitat patches would need to be described accordingly. Such detailed analyses are likely of most interest to users with specific seasonal or phenology questions in mind, and they would require much additional data. For users unwilling or unable to devote the time and costs necessary for such detailed analysis, these effects must be kept in mind when considering the simpler analysis of one time in midsummer.

In all cases, it is especially important that users remember that the habitat values calculated by the FRESH system (Deer Days/ha) are indexes that reflect the total food supply—an integration of its total quantity and quality relative to the specified nutritional requirements of deer at the particular time of analysis. Differences among habitats are consistent with their differences in total food resources. Although total food resources determine a habitat's capacity to produce and sustain deer, they are not a useful predictor of animal behavior. Just as population density can be a misleading indicator of habitat quality (Van Horne 1983), so too can food and habitat preferences be misleading about relative carrying capacities (Hobbs and Hanley 1990). Quantity and quality of food resources are not substitutable for each other in herbivore diets, especially for ruminants; therefore, optimal food and habitat selection should be expected to vary with population density (which is not a measurable habitat feature) (Hobbs and Hanley 1990). The FRESH system does not provide a basis for predicting optimal food or habitat choice (behavior) at any level of population density other than a completely saturated landscape exactly at its food capacity at that time.

Acknowledgments

We thank the following people for their careful reviews of earlier draft manuscripts: Elizabeth C. Cole, John G. Cook, Mary A. Friberg, David R. Klein, Lisa A. Shipley, and Beatrice Van Horne. We also thank Kenneth J. Raedeke for his continued interest and help with this project throughout its long evolution. Richard Harris and Ron Wolfe of Sealaska Corporation were instrumental in identifying the need for this project and have been supportive throughout. We also appreciate the interest and support from Forrest Cole and Patricia O'Connor of the Tongass National Forest in the use of the system.

English Equivalents

When you know:	Multiply by:	To get:
Centimeters (cm)	0.394	Inches
Meters (m)	3.28	Feet
Hectares (ha)	2.47	Acres
Square meters (m^2)	10.76	Square feet
Grams (g)	0.0352	Ounces
Kilograms (kg)	2.205	Pounds
Kilojoules (kJ)	0.948	British Thermal Units (BTU)
Kilojoules per gram (kJ/g)	26.932	BTU/ounce
Degrees Celsius (°C)	1.8°C + 32	Degrees Fahrenheit
Jigger (j)	1.500	Ounces

Literature Cited

Alaback, P.B. 1986. Biomass regression equations for understory plants in coastal Alaska: effects of species and sampling design on estimates. Northwest Science. 60: 90–103.

Barbour, M.G.; Burk, J.H.; Pitts, W.D. 1987. Terrestrial plant ecology, second edition. Menlo Park, CA: Benjamin/Cummings Publishing Company, Inc. 634 p.

Caughley, G. 1977. Analysis of vertebrate populations. New York, NY: John Wiley and Sons. 234 p.

Cole, E.C.; Hanley, T.A.; Newton, M. 2010. Influence of precommercial thinning on understory vegetation of young-growth Sitka spruce forests in southeastern Alaska. Canadian Journal of Forest Research. 40: 619–628.

Cook, J.G.; Johnson, B.K.; Cook, R.C.; Riggs, R.A.; DelCurto, T.; Bryant, L.D.; Irwin, L.L. 2004. Effects of summer-autumn nutrition and parturition on reproduction and survival of elk. Wildlife Monographs. 155: 1–61.

Doerr, J.G.; DeGayner, E.J.; Ith, G. 2005. Winter habitat selection by Sitka black-tailed deer. Journal of Wildlife Management. 69: 322–331.

Farmer, C.J. 2002. Survival and habitat selection of Sitka black-tailed deer (*Odocoileus hemionus sitkensis*) in a fragmented coastal temperate rainforest. Syracuse, NY: State University of New York. Ph.D. dissertation.

Gillingham, M.P.; Parker, K.L.; Hanley, T.A. 1997. Forage intake by large generalist herbivores in a natural forest environment: bout dynamics. Canadian Journal of Zoology. 75: 1118–1128.

Gillingham, M.P.; Parker, K.L.; Hanley, T.A. 2000. Partial consumption of shield fern, *Dryopteris dilatata*, rhizomes by black-tailed deer, *Odocoileus hemionus*, and its potential implications. Canadian Field-Naturalist. 114: 21–25.

Hanley, T.A. 1984. Relationships between Sitka black-tailed deer and their habitat. Gen. Tech. Rep. PNW-168. Portland, OR: U.S. Department of Agriculture, Forest Service, Pacific Northwest Forest and Range Experiment Station. 21 p.

Hanley, T.A. 1997. A nutritional view of understanding and complexity in the problem of diet selection by deer (Cervidae). Oikos. 79: 209–218.

Hanley, T.A.; Deal, R.L.; Orlikowska, E.H. 2006. Relations between red alder composition and understory vegetation in young mixed forests of southeast Alaska. Canadian Journal of Forest Research. 36: 738–748.

Hanley, T.A.; McKendrick, J.D. 1983. Seasonal changes in chemical composition and nutritive value of native forages in a spruce-hemlock forest, southeastern Alaska. Res. Pap. PNW-312. Portland, OR: U.S. Department of Agriculture, Forest Service, Pacific Northwest Forest and Range Experiment Station. 41 p.

Hanley, T.A.; McKendrick, J.D. 1985. Potential nutritional limitations for black-tailed deer in a spruce-hemlock forest, southeastern Alaska. Journal of Wildlife Management. 49: 103–114.

Hanley, T.A.; Robbins, C.T.; Hagerman, A.E.; McArthur, C. 1992. Predicting digestible protein and digestible dry matter in tannin-containing forages consumed by ruminants. Ecology. 73: 537–541.

Hanley, T.A.; Robbins, C.T.; Spalinger, D.E. 1989. Forest habitats and the nutritional ecology of Sitka black-tailed deer: a research synthesis with implications for forest management. Gen. Tech. Rep. PNW-GTR-230. Portland, OR: U.S. Department of Agriculture, Forest Service, Pacific Northwest Research Station. 52 p.

Hanley, T.A.; Rogers, J.J. 1989. Estimating carrying capacity with simultaneous nutritional constraints. Research Note PNW-RN-485. Portland, OR: U.S. Department of Agriculture, Forest Service, Pacific Northwest Research Station. 29 p.

Hanley, T.A.; Rose, C.L. 1987. Influence of overstory on snow depth and density in hemlock-spruce stands: implications for management of deer habitat in southeastern Alaska. Res. Note PNW-RN-459. Portland, OR: U.S. Department of Agriculture, Forest Service, Pacific Northwest Research Station. 11 p.

Hanley, T.A.; Spalinger, D.E.; Hanley, K.A.; Schoen, J.W. 1985. Relationships between fecal and rumen analyses for deer diet assessments in southeastern Alaska. Northwest Science. 59: 10–16.

Harestad, A.S.; Bunnell, F.L. 1981. Prediction of snow-water equivalents in coniferous forests. Canadian Journal of Forest Research. 11: 854–857.

Hobbs, N.T. 1989. Linking energy balance to survival in mule deer: development and test of a simulation model. Wildlife Monographs. 101: 1–39.

Hobbs, N.T.; Gross, J.E.; Shipley, L.A.; Spalinger, D.E.; Wunder, B.A. 2003. Herbivore functional response in heterogeneous environments: a contest among models. Ecology. 84: 666–681.

Hobbs, N.T.; Hanley, T.A. 1990. Habitat evaluation: Do use/availability data reflect carrying capacity? Journal of Wildllife Management. 54: 515–522.

Hobbs, N.T.; Swift, D.M. 1985. Estimates of habitat carrying capacity incorporating explicit nutritional constraints. Journal of Wildlife Management. 49: 814–822.

Hovey, F.W. 1987. Shrub burial by snow deposition in immature coastal forests: a review and recommendations. Pub. IWIFR-35. Victoria, BC: BC Ministry of Environment and Parks and B.C. Ministry of Forests and Lands. 20 p.

Hovey, F.W.; Harestad, A.S. 1992. Estimating effects of snow on shrub availability for black-tailed deer in southwestern British Columbia. Wildlife Society Bulletin. 20: 308–313.

Hudson, R.J.; White, R.G. 1985. Bioenergetics of wild herbivores. Boca Raton, FL: CRC Press. 314 p.

Jenkins, K.J.; Happe, P.J.; Wright, R.G. 1990. Evaluating above-snow browse availability using nonlinear regressions. Wildlife Society Bulletin. 18: 49–55.

Johnstone, J.; Russell, D.E.; Griffith, B. 2002. Variations in plant forage quality in the range of the Porcupine Caribou Herd. Rangifer. 22(1): 83–92.

Kirchhoff, M.D.; Schoen, J.W. 1987. Forest cover and snow: implications for deer habitat in southeast Alaska. Journal of Wildlife Management. 51: 28–33.

Klein, D.R. 1964. Range-related differences in growth of deer reflected in skeletal ratios. Journal of Mammalogy. 45: 226–235.

Klein, D.R. 1965. Ecology of deer range in Alaska. Ecological Monographs. 35: 259–284.

Klein, D.R.; Olson, S.T. 1960. Natural mortality patterns of deer in southeast Alaska. Journal of Wildlife Management. 24: 80–88.

Leslie, D.M., Jr.; Starkey, E.E.; Vavra, M. 1984. Elk and deer diets in old-growth forests in western Washington. Journal of Wildlife Management. 48: 762–775.

Lewis, S.W. 1992. Relationships between deer and vegetation on Coronation Island, southeastern Alaska. Fairbanks, AK: University of Alaska Fairbanks. 103 p. M.S. thesis.

Lewis, S.W. 1994. Fecal and rumen analyses in relation to temporal variation in black-tailed deer diets. Journal of Wildlife Management. 58: 53–58.

Long, R.A.; Muir, J.D.; Rachlow, J.L.; Kie, J.G. 2009. A comparison of two modeling approaches for evaluating wildlife-habitat relationships. Journal of Wildlife Management. 73: 294–302.

Manly, B.F.J.; McDonald, L.L.; Thomas, D.L. 1993. Resource selection by animals. Statistical design and analysis for field studies. London: Chapman and Hall. 240 p.

May, R.M. 1973. Stability and complexity in model ecosystems. Princeton, NJ: Princeton University Press. 292 p.

McArt, S.H.; Spalinger, D.E.; Kennish, J.M.; Collins, W.B. 2006. A modified method for determining tannin-protein precipitation capacity using accelerated solvent extraction (ASE) and microplate gel filtration. Journal of Chemical Ecology. 32: 1367–1377.

McArthur, C.; Robbins, C.T.; Hagerman, A.E.; Hanley, T.A. 1993. Diet selection by a ruminant generalist browser in relation to plant chemistry. Canadian Journal of Zoology. 71: 2236–2243.

McClellan, M.H.; DeSanto, T.L. [In press]. Tongass-Wide Young-Growth Studies: study plan and establishment report. Gen. Tech. Rep. Portland, OR: U.S. Department of Agriculture, Forest Service, Pacific Northwest Research Station.

McCullough, D.R. 1979. The George Reserve deer herd: population ecology of a K-selected species. Ann Arbor, MI: University of Michigan Press. 271 p.

Moen, A.A. 1973. Wildlife ecology: an analytical approach. San Francisco, CA: W.H. Freeman and Company. 458 p.

Mould, E.D.; Robbins, C.T. 1981. Evaluation of detergent analysis in estimating nutritional value of browse. Journal of Wildlife Management. 45: 937–947.

National Research Council. 2007. Nutrient requirements of small ruminants: sheep, goats, cervids, and New World camelids. Washington, DC: National Academies Press. 362 p.

Olson, S.T. 1952. Winter mortality of black-tailed deer, factors affecting, extent and frequency. Fed. Aid. In: Wildl. Rest., Proj. W-3-R-7, Work Plan E. Juneau, AK: Alaska Department of Fish and Game. 18 p.

Olson, S.T.; Klein, D.R. 1959. Sitka black-tailed deer studies. Fed. Aid. In: Wildl. Rest., Serv. Job. Completion Rep. 13(4). Proj. W-3-R-13, Work Plan E. Juneau, AK: Alaska Department of Fish and Game. 37 p.

Parker, K.L. 1988. Effects of heat, cold, and rain on coastal black-tailed deer. Canadian Journal of Zoology. 66: 2475–2483.

Parker, K.L.; Gillingham, M.P. 1990. Estimates of critical thermal environments for mule deer. Journal of Range Management. 43: 73–81.

Parker, K.L.; Gillingham, M.P.; Hanley, T.A.; Robbins, C.T. 1993. Seasonal patterns in body mass, body composition, and water transfer rates of free-ranging and captive black-tailed deer (□□ocoi□eus hemionus sit□ensis) in Alaska. Canadian Journal of Zoology. 71: 1397–1404.

Parker, K.L.; Gillingham, M.P.; Hanley, T.A.; Robbins, C.T. 1996. Foraging efficiency: energy expenditure versus energy gain in free-ranging black-tailed deer. Canadian Journal of Zoology. 74: 442–450.

Parker, K.L.; Gillingham, M.P.; Hanley, T.A.; Robbins, C.T. 1999. Energy and protein balance of free-ranging black-tailed deer in a natural forest environment. Wildlife Monographs. 143: 1–48.

Parker, K.L.; Robbins, C.T. 1984. Thermoregulation in mule deer and elk. Canadian Journal of Zoology. 62: 1409–1422.

Parker, K.L.; Robbins, C.T.; Hanley, T.A. 1984. Energy expenditures for locomotion by mule deer and elk. Journal of Wildlife Management. 48: 474–488.

Pielou, E.C. 1977. Mathematical ecology. New York, NY: John Wiley & Sons. 385 p.

Pierce, R.A., II. 1981. The food habits of the Sitka black-tailed deer on Prince of Wales Island, Alaska. Mississippi State, MS: Mississippi State University. 30 p. M.S. thesis.

Robbins, C.T. 1987. Digestibility of an arboreal lichen (□ectoria sarmentosa) by mule deer. Journal of Range Management. 40: 491–492.

Robbins, C.T. 1993. Wildlife feeding and nutrition, second edition. New York, NY: Academic Press. 352 p.

Robbins, C.T.; Hagerman, A.E.; Austin, P.J.; McArthur, C.; Hanley, T.A. 1991. Variation in mammalian physiological responses to a condensed tannin and its ecological implications. Journal of Mammalogy. 72: 480–486.

Robbins, C.T.; Hanley, T.A.; Hagerman, A.E.; Hjeljord, O.; Baker, D.L.; Schwartz, C.C.; Mautz, W.W. 1987a. Role of tannins in defending plants against ruminants: reduction in protein availability. Ecology. 68: 98–107.

Robbins, C.T.; Mole, S.; Hagerman, A.E.; Hanley, T.A. 1987b. Role of tannins in defending plants against ruminants: reduction in dry matter digestion? Ecology. 68: 1606–1615.

Robbins, C.T.; Moen, A.N. 1975. Uterine composition and growth in pregnant white-tailed deer. Journal of Wildlife Management. 39: 684–691.

Rosenthal, G.A.; Janzen, D.H. 1979. Herbivores: their interaction with secondary plant metabolites. New York, NY: Academic Press. 718 p.

Sadleir, R.M.F.S. 1980. Energy and protein in relation to growth of suckling black-tailed deer fawns. Canadian Journal of Zoology. 58: 1347–1354.

Schoen, J.W.; Kirchhoff, M.D. 1985. Seasonal distribution and home range patterns of Sitka black-tailed deer on Admiralty Island, Southeast Alaska. Journal of Wildlife Management. 49: 96–103.

Schoen, J.W.; Kirchhoff, M.D. 1990. Seasonal habitat use by Sitka black-tailed deer on Admiralty Island, Alaska. Journal of Wildlife Management. 54: 371–378.

Shipley, L.A.; Gross, J.E.; Spalinger, D.E.; Hobbs, N.T.; Wunder, B.A. 1994. The scaling of intake rate in mammalian herbivores. American Naturalist. 143: 1055–1082.

Shipley, L.A.; Spalinger, D.E. 1992. Mechanics of browsing in dense food patches: effects of plant and animal morphology on intake rate. Canadian Journal of Zoology. 70: 1743–1752.

Shipley, L.A.; Spalinger, D.E. 1995. Influence of size and density of browse patches on intake rates and foraging decisions of young moose and white-tailed deer. Oecologia. 104: 112–121.

Shipley, L.A.; Spalinger, D.E.; Gross, J.E.; Hobbs, N.T.; Wunder, B.A. 1996. The dynamics and scaling of foraging velocity and encounter rate in mammalian herbivores. Functional Ecology. 10: 234–244.

Short, H.L. 1981. Nutrition and metabolism. In: Wallmo, O.C., ed. Mule and black-tailed deer of North America. Lincoln, NE: University of Nebraska Press. 99–127.

Snedecor, G.W.; Cochran, W.G. 1967. Statistical methods. 6th ed. Ames, IA: Iowa State University Press. 593 p.

Spalinger, D.E.; Collins, W.B.; Hanley, T.A.; Cassara, N.E.; Carnahan, A.M. 2010. The impact of tannins on protein, dry matter, and energy digestion in moose (*Alces alces*). Canadian Journal of Zoology. 88: 977–987.

Spalinger, D.E.; Hanley, T.A.; Robbins, C.T. 1988. Analysis of the functional response in foraging in the Sitka black-tailed deer. Ecology. 69: 1166–1175.

Spalinger, D.E.; Hobbs, N.T. 1992. Mechanisms of foraging in mammalian herbivores: new models of functional response. American Naturalist. 140: 325–348.

Spalinger, D.E.; Robbins, C.T. 1992. The dynamics of particle flow in the rumen of mule deer (☐*ocoi*☐*eus hemionus hemionus*) and elk (☐*er*☐*us e*☐*a*☐*hus ne*☐*soni*). Physiological Zoology. 65: 379–402.

Spalinger, D.E.; Robbins, C.T.; Hanley, T.A. 1986. The assessment of handling time in ruminants: the effect of plant chemical and physical structure on the rate of breakdown of plant particles in the rumen of mule deer and elk. Canadian Journal of Zoology. 64: 312–321.

Spalinger, D.E.; Robbins, C.T.; Hanley, T.A. 1993. Adaptive rumen function in elk (☐*er*☐*us e*☐*a*☐*hus ne*☐*soni*) and mule deer (☐*ocoi*☐*eus hemionus hemionus*). Canadian Journal of Zoology. 71: 601–610.

Stoddart, L.A.; Smith, A.D.; Box, T.W. 1975. Range management, third edition. New York, NY: McGraw-Hill. 532 p.

U.S. Department of Agriculture, Natural Resources Conservation Service [USDA NRCS]. Snow course survey data. http://www.ak.nrcs.usda.gov/ Snow/snowsites.html and http://www.ambcs.org/pub/sc_sum_ak/ SNOWCOURSE.HTM.

U.S. Department of Commerce, National Oceanographic and Atmospheric Administration [USDC NOAA]. Juneau International Airport weather observations. National Climate Data Center. http://hurricane.ncdc.noaa.gov/ dly/DLY.

Vales, D.J. 1986. Functional relationships between salal understory and forest overstory. Vancouver, BC: University of British Columbia. 164 p. M.S. thesis.

Van Horne, B. 1983. Density as a misleading indicator of habitat quality. Journal of Wildlife Management. 47: 893–901.

Van Horne, B.; Hanley T.A.; Cates, R.G.; McKendrick, J.D.; Horner, J.D. 1988. Influence of seral stage and season on leaf chemistry of southeastern Alaska deer forage. Canadian Journal Forest Research. 18: 90–99.

Van Soest, P.J. 1982. Nutritional ecology of the ruminant. Corvallis, OR: O&B Books. 374 p.

Wallmo, O.C.; Carpenter, L.H.; Regelin, W.L.; Gill, R.B.; Baker, D.L. 1977. Evaluation of deer habitat on a nutritional basis. Journal of Range Management. 30: 122–127.

White, K.S.; Pendleton, G.W.; Hood, E. 2009. Effects of snow on Sitka black-tailed deer browse availability and nutritional carrying capacity in southeastern Alaska. Journal of Wildlife Management. 73: 481–487.

White, R.G. 1983. Foraging patterns and their multiplier effects on productivity of northern ungulates. Oikos. 40: 377–384.

White, T.C.R. 1993. The inadequate environment. Nitrogen and the abundance of animals. Berlin: Springer-Verlag. 425 p.

Wickstrom, M.L.; Robbins, C.T.; Hanley, T.A.; Spalinger, D.E.; Parish, S.M. 1984. Food intake and foraging energetics of elk and mule deer. Journal of Wildlife Management. 48: 1285–1301.

Yeo, J.J.; Peek, J.M. 1992. Habitat selection by female Sitka black-tailed deer in logged forests of southeastern Alaska. Journal of Wildlife Management. 56: 253–261.

Zaborske, R.R.; Hauver, R.N.; McClellan, M.H.; Hanley, T.A. 2002. Vegetation development following commercial thinning in southeast Alaska: preliminary results from the second-growth management area demonstration project. In: Parker, S.; Hummel, S.S., eds. Beyond 2001: a silvicultural odyssey of sustaining terrestrial and aquatic ecosystems. Proceedings of the 2001 national silviculture workshop. Gen. Tech. Rep. PNW-GTR-564. Portland, OR: U.S. Department of Agriculture, Forest Service, Pacific Northwest Research Station: 74–82.

Appendix 1: Suggested Field and Laboratory Methods for Obtaining Original Data for Forage Biomass and Nutritional Quality

Field data requirements for Forage Resource Evaluation System for Habitat—Deer (FRESH-Deer, a food-based system for quantitatively evaluating habitat quality for deer) are the following: (1) identification of "habitat types" (plant community types) and "forages" (plant species and parts), (2) estimates of available forage biomass and overstory canopy coverage of each habitat type, and (3) estimates of nutritional values of each forage for each time of year to be analyzed. All values of biomass and nutritional data in the current linked databases of FRESH-Deer are for analyses focused on early July for summer and early February for winter. Similarly, parameter values in the current snow submodel are for February 1. The user may elect to use those same timeframes for analysis, or select different times. If different times are chosen, then it will be important to adjust the recommended metabolic requirements (table 1) accordingly, too.

Frequently, the user will want to input their own original habitat type and forage availability data but will not want to collect original forage nutritional data. In that case, they can use the linked forage nutritional database for nutritional estimates (app. 2), as long as they input their forage data identified by plant codes (app. 3). Any forages not included in the current list of plant codes will need to be identified as "other" forages (see app. 3) or will need original nutritional data.

Identification of Habitat Types

For most stand-level analyses, the "habitat type" will be obvious. It will be simply the plant community being analyzed. Examples are experimental treatments, silviculture treatments, and other a priori defined plant community types. Sometimes, questions arise about whether various a priori plant community types differ enough to require classification as different habitat types or whether they should be combined as the same habitat type. The answer to that question usually depends □□ □□□ □□□□□□□□□□□ □□□□□□□□□□□□□□□□□□□□□ □□□□□□ □□ □□□□□□ □□□□□□ □□□-munity type, then each stand can be evaluated with FRESH-Deer, and the resulting Deer Days/Ha values of each type can be analyzed in an analysis of variance and comparison of means, which will identify similar from dissimilar community types in relation to deer food resources. Similar community types could be combined into one habitat type. Alternatively, similarities in vegetation pattern can be analyzed directly with any of various multivariate analytical techniques as described below.

When plant community types or habitat types are not obvious or defined a priori, then they must be identified and described by the user. This is a typical plant community ecology problem for which the user can consult various textbooks (e.g., Barbour et al. 1987). Choices of habitat types will likely depend on existing plant community data sources and maps. Analysis of vegetation gradients of similarity/dissimilarity will likely be by various multivariate ordination techniques and gradient analyses.

The current geographic information system (GIS) application for landscape-level analysis requires that habitat types be defined and that each be described in terms of its mean forage-specific biomass availabilities (ovendry kilograms per hectare [kg/ha] of each forage) and mean overstory canopy coverage (percentage). The habitat types will be mapped in GIS space, and all pixels within a given habitat type will be assigned the vegetation of that type.

Vegetation Data and Sampling Procedures

The user must identify their "available forages" (see boxes 3 and 4, p. 8 for definitions of "available" and "forages"). Forages are the plant species eaten by deer, which usually include virtually all plant species. They are also differentiated by plant part when the parts differ substantially in their nutritional quality. For example, leaves are considered separately from twigs for shrub species. Similarly, if a species occurs in widely different phenological growth stages (e.g., young leaves and old, desiccated leaves) simultaneously, it would be best to treat the phenological stages as different forages. We consider only current annual growth as "forage," so older stems of shrubs and trees are not included; but that decision is up to the user. "Availability" of a forage is influenced by its height profile (minimum and maximum heights aboveground, centimeters) specified by the user and its burial by snow in the snow submodel. Some users prefer to limit the maximum available height to what can be reached by a foraging deer, whereas others prefer not to do that, assuming that greater heights can be accessed when deer walk on top of firm snowpacks. The user also must identify how much of each forage remains available in snow-free winter, as a percentage of its summer biomass (e.g., shrub twigs and evergreen leaves may be given values of 100 percent, whereas deciduous leaves are 0 percent). That value is used in converting summer data sets to winter data sets. The user also must specify a "maximum percentage in the solution set" for each forage they choose to limit in that way (see "Factors Affecting Nutrition and Palatability" in general discussion of FRESH); that forage-specific constraint should be based on known diet composition data from free-ranging deer.

Biomass (ovendry kg/ha) of each available forage must be determined for each stand (stand-level analysis) to be analyzed or each habitat type (landscape-level analysis) on the landscape. Biomass sampling is another classic plant community ecology problem (see Barbour et al. 1987 or similar text for details). If sampling is conducted in summer (e.g., late June through early August), then biomass availability in winter can be calculated by FRESH-Deer through the "convert summer to winter" routine (box 5). Although most statistical analyses assume random sampling for determining biomass within a plant community, most plant ecologists find efficiency is increased markedly by stratified systematic sampling, whereby the community is sampled systematically (e.g., sample quadrats placed at given intervals along a measuring tape or transect) and unique patches of vegetation are stratified (sampled separately). Biomass of each forage within each quadrat is measured either directly by clipping and weighing (with representative subsamples ovendried at 100 °C for dry-weight correction), or estimated indirectly by using allometric regression equations to convert measures of plants (e.g., canopy cover, basal stem diameter) to biomass (see Alaback 1986 for examples of allometric regressions for a wide range of southeastern Alaska species). Users who opt for allometric regressions should be aware, however, that such relations tend to be site-specific (Alaback 1986); thus separate regressions for the same species may be needed for different silviculture treatments, or types of old-growth forest, for example.

Forage Nutritional Analysis

FRESH-Deer operates on user-specified constraints for two forage nutritional factors. We have emphasized minimum requirements for digestible protein (DP) and digestible energy (DE) as the two most important constraints. In an environment with a known mineral deficiency for deer (e.g., a phosphorus deficiency), the minimum requirement for that mineral could be substituted for the DP constraint by ages. However, for the usual situation, DP and DE will be the prime factors. Digestible energy is calculated as the product of gross energy concentration (kJ/g) and dry matter digestibility (DMD, g/100 g or percentage); of those two, gross energy is much less variable than is DMD (Robbins 1993), so oftentimes, sampling effort is focused on DMD and a constant value is assumed for gross energy. The focus on DMD is usually done to maximize the number of samples that can be analyzed within a total budget available for laboratory analyses. FRESH-Deer can work with either DMD or DE as the energy constraint.

Forage samples should be collected in the field from plants within the habitats being analyzed and at the same time of the year that will be the focus of the FRESH analysis. We usually focus on early July for summer and early February for winter analyses. Samples must be collected for each forage at both of those times. Samples

Usually, this is done by collecting a composite sample of a given forage at any one

░░░░ ░░░ ░░░ ░░░░░░░░ ░░░ ░░░░░░░ ░░░░░░░ ░░░░░░░ ░░░░░░░░░░ ░░░░░░░░

Vaccinium spp., differ significantly in their DP and DMD values as a function of the light environment (shade) of their habitat (Hanley et al. 1992, McArthur et al. 1993, Van Horne et al. 1988), and they should be treated separately.

Samples (5 to 10 g dry weight) should be clipped and bagged as quickly as possible and, ideally, frozen immediately on dry ice and kept frozen with dry ice until freeze-drying as soon as possible. Once freeze-dried, the sample can be kept in the dark in a sealed jar at room temperature more or less indefinitely. Immediate freezing at ultra-cold temperatures stops all metabolic activity in the plant tissue; freeze-drying dries the frozen sample in a way that prevents chemical interaction of compounds mixed by the breaking of frozen vacuoles within the plant cells. Although freezing with dry ice and subsequent freeze-drying is the ideal, such treatment often is highly impractical in remote field situations. Therefore, the next best alternative is to bag the sample, keep it out of direct sun, and **ovendry** ░░░░ 40 °C as soon as possible. Drying at either cooler (20°) or warmer (60°) temperatures is not advisable (Mould and Robbins 1981). If samples are to be ground before shipping to a laboratory for analysis, they should be ground dried in a Wiley Mill with 20-mesh screen.

For laboratory analyses, we strongly recommend the procedures and equations described by Robbins et al. (1987a, 1987b) and Hanley et al. 1992, although the BSA-precipitation can be conducted by the modified method of McArt et al. (2006) to reduce costs. Of interest to users in southeastern Alaska is that Hanley et al. tested the equations with in vivo feeding trials using Sitka black-tailed deer (*Odocoileus hemionus sitkensis* Merriam). Other users may be interested to know that the Robbins et al. equations were developed from in vivo feeding trials with several deer species and have recently been found to be robust even for Alaska moose (*Alces alces* Linnaeus) (Spalinger et al. 2010). Digestible protein is estimated as a function of "crude protein" (total nitrogen concentration times 6.25) and protein-precipitating capacity of plant tannins. For tannin-free graminoids (most graminoids), DP can be estimated as a function of crude protein alone. Digestible dry matter is estimated as a function of sequential fiber analyses and DP reduction by tannins. The Robbins et al. and Hanley et al. papers provide all necessary equations for calculating DP and DMD and interpreting the results. Sequential fiber analysis has the strong advantages of being tied directly to in vivo digestion

░░░░░░░░ ░░░░░░░░░ ░░░░░ ░░░░░░░ ░░░░░░░ ░░░ ░░░░░░░ ░░░░░░░

the calculated DMD value through its component parts. We caution against using in vitro digestion results for DMD, because in vitro results are simply an index of

DMD (they can vary with source of rumen fluid, for example, and the 48-hour time period is arbitrary) and are not tied directly to in vivo results from deer with strong predictive equations. In vitro DMD is usually less expensive than the sequential fiber method and may be used as an estimate in the absence of sequential fiber data, but we believe the greater value of the sequential fiber technique is worth the

analyses, so they will need to contract with a commercial lab. Although we make no recommendation, nor do we imply a recommendation, one laboratory that has been performing these and similar analyses for more than 30 years is the Wildlife Habitat Nutrition Laboratory at Washington State University in Pullman, Washington.

Appendix 2: Nutritional Data (mean ± standard deviation) in the Nutritional Database

Species/part	Source	Summer		Winter	
		DMD	DP	DMD	DP
		- - - - - - - - - - - - - - - - - *Percent* - - - - - - - - - - - - - - - - - -			
Ferns:					
Adiantum pedatus	1	52.7 ± 8.5[a]	10.3 ± 2.1	—	—
Athyrium filix-femina	1	55.7	14.6	—	—
	2	51.1	10.2	—	—
	Mean	53.4 ± 3.3	12.4 ± 3.1	—	—
Blechnum spicant	1	50.5	7.4	(50.5)[b]	(7.4)
	2	46.9	5.7	64.6	5.6
	Mean	48.7 ± 2.5	6.6 ± 1.2	57.6 ± 10.0	6.5 ± 1.3
Dryopteris expansa	1	55.2	9.6	—	—
dilatata	2	49.4	7.8	66.2	10.4
dilatata	3	25.1	6.7	48.2	7.3
	Mean	43.2 ± 16.0	8.0 ± 1.5	57.2 ± 12.7	8.9 ± 2.2
Gymnocarpium dryopteris	1	55.9 ± 9.0	8.0 ± 1.7	—	—
Polystichum spp.	1	47.5 ± 7.6	6.0 ± 1.2	(47.5) ± 9.4	(6.0) ± 1.3
Mean "ferns"		50.2 ± 4.6	8.6 ± 2.4	54.1 ± 5.7	7.1 ± 1.6
Forbs:					
Coptis asplenifolia	1	53.1	6.1	(53.1)	(6.1)
	2	71.9	6.1	78.3	5.9
	3	63.6	5.9	72.4	4.1
	Mean	62.2 ± 9.4	6.0 ± 0.1	67.9 ± 13.2	5.4 ± 1.1
Cornus canadensis	1	62.3	6.3	(62.3)	(6.3)
	2	59.3	7.2	72.2	7.2
	3	58.4	8.4	75.6	6.0
	Mean	60.0 ± 2.0	7.3 ± 1.1	70.0 ± 6.9	6.5 ± 0.6
Epilobium angustifolium	4	48.2	0.5	—	—
	5	65.4	5.4	—	—
	Mean	56.8 ± 12.2	3.0 ± 3.5	—	—
Fauria crista-galli	3	78.6 ± 12.3	11.3 ± 3.3	—	—
Listera spp.	3	72.7 ± 11.4	9.0 ± 2.6	—	—
Lysichiton americanus	1	58.4	17.8	—	—
	2	50.4	24.8	—	—
	3	75.5	26.0	—	—
	Mean	61.4 ± 12.8	22.9 ± 4.4	—	—
Maianthemum dilatatum	1	63.5	8.4	—	—
	2	72.3	8.9	—	—
	3	77.4	4.5	—	—
	Mean	71.1 ± 7.0	7.3 ± 2.4	—	—

Appendix 2: Nutritional Data (mean ± standard deviation) in the Nutritional Database *(continued)*

Species/part	Source	Summer		Winter	
		DMD	DP	DMD	DP
		------------------ *Percent* ------------------			
Monesis uniflora	1	67.5	10.1	(67.5)	(10.1)
	3	66.1	6.1	62.2	6.6
	Mean	66.8 ± 1.0	8.1 ± 2.8	64.9 ± 3.7	8.4 ± 2.5
Potentilla spp.	2	55.7 ± 8.7	4.5 ± 1.3	—	—
Prenanthes alata	2	69.4 ± 10.9	11.8 ± 3.4	—	—
Rubus pedatus	1	62.6	6.2	(62.6)	(6.2)
	2	74.3	8.6	75.0	8.0
	3	46.3	6.4	54.3	5.7
	Mean	61.1 ± 14.1	7.1 ± 1.3	64.0 ± 10.4	6.6 ± 1.2
Streptopus spp.	3	69.8	10.0	—	—
amplexifolius	1	56.1	13.4	—	—
	2	86.2	9.2	—	—
roseus	1	57.4	11.5	—	—
streptopoides	1	64.8	9.4	—	—
	2	73.6	9.6	—	—
	Mean	68.0 ± 11.2	10.5 ± 1.6	—	—
Tiarella trifoliata	2	66.3	8.4	65.7	6.9
	3	43.5	7.6	61.3	5.1
	Mean	54.9 ± 16.1	8.0 ± 0.6	63.5 ± 3.1	6.0 ± 1.3
Mean "forbs"		64.5 ± 7.2	9.0 ± 4.9	66.1 ± 2.8	6.6 ± 1.1
Graminoids:					
Luzula parviflora	1	62.1 ± 8.4[c]	3.8 ± 2.3	—	—
Bromus sitchensis	1	65.3 ± 8.9	8.8 ± 5.2	—	—
Carex lyngbyaei	3	42.0 ± 5.7	0.1 ± 0.1	—	—
Carex mertensii	1	63.4 + 8.6	9.2 ± 5.5	—	—
Carex spp.	2	55.7 ± 7.6	9.2 ± 5.5	—	—
Deschampsia caespitosa	3	63.3 ± 8.6	3.4 ± 2.0	—	—
Elymus arenarius	2	60.3 ± 8.2	6.7 ± 4.0	—	—
Mean "graminoids"		58.9 ± 8.0	5.9 ± 3.5	—	—
Shrubs:					
Alnus sinuata leaves (eaten only very sparingly)	2	73.4 ± 7.2	13.0 ± 3.7	—	—
Empetrum nigrum leaves	3	(29.9) ± 2.9	(1.4) ± 0.4	29.9 ± 2.9	1.4 ± 0.4
Ledum palustra	3	(39.9) ± 3.9	(2.5) ± 0.7	39.9 ± 3.9	2.5 ± 0.7

Appendix 2: Nutritional Data (mean ± standard deviation) in the Nutritional Database *(continued)*

Species/part	Source	Summer		Winter	
		DMD	DP	DMD	DP
		- - - - - - - - - - - - - - - - - *Percent* - - - - - - - - - - - - - - - - - - -			
Menziesia ferruginea leaves	1	57.8	10.0	—	—
	2	56.7	7.5	—	—
	3	46.6	7.7	—	—
	Mean	53.7 ± 6.2	8.4 ± 1.4	—	—
Menziesia ferruginea twigs	1	45.1	2.1	—	—
	2	54.5	9.1	34.1	1.9
	3	21.2	0.3	27.1	2.6
	Mean	40.3 ± 17.2	3.8 ± 4.6	30.6 ± 4.9	2.3 ± 0.5
Oplopanax horridus leaves	1	61.0	13.8	—	—
	2	70.1	8.5	—	—
	3	74.0	11.7	—	—
	Mean	68.4 ± 6.7	11.3 ± 2.7	—	—
Ribes bracteosum leaves	1	57.4 ± 5.6	10.0 ± 2.9	—	—
Ribes laxiflorum leaves	1	67.4 ± 6.6	10.3 ± 3.0	—	—
Rubus spectabilis leaves	1	59.6	14.3	—	—
	2	63.1	16.0	—	—
	3	43.3	8.0	—	—
	4	53.9	6.7	—	—
	5	64.9	10.1	—	—
	Mean	56.9 ± 8.7	11.0 ± 4.0	—	—
Salix sitchensis leaves	4	55.7	8.1	—	—
	5	55.0	6.3	—	—
Salix spp. leaves	5	63.0	10.0	—	—
	Mean	57.9 ± 4.4	8.1 ± 1.9	—	—
Sambucus racemosa leaves	1	59.3	17.0	—	—
	4	71.3	23.5	—	—
	5	71.5	16.0	—	—
	Mean	67.4 ± 7.0	18.8 ± 4.1	—	—
Vaccinium ovalifolium/alaskensis					
Leaves, forest	1	44.0	12.9	—	—
	2	43.0	9.4	—	—
	3	45.8	10.8	—	—
	4	54.0	9.1	—	—
	5	47.7	5.7	—	—
	Mean	46.9 ± 4.4	9.6 ± 2.6	—	—
Leaves, sunny habitat	1	54.5	10.8	—	—
	4	52.5	5.0	—	—
	5	55.2	5.0	—	—
	Mean	54.1 ± 1.4	6.9 ± 3.3	—	—

Appendix 2: Nutritional Data (mean ± standard deviation) in the Nutritional Database *(continued)*

Species/part	Source	Summer DMD	Summer DP	Winter DMD	Winter DP
		- - - - - - - - - - - - - - - - - *Percent* - - - - - - - - - - - - - - - - -			
Twigs	1	30.8	2.7	(30.8)	(2.7)
	2	—	—	51.9	4.4
	3	27.8	2.5	36.1	4.8
	Mean	29.3 ± 2.1	2.6 ± 0.1	39.6 ± 11.0	4.0 ± 1.1
Vaccinium parvifolium					
Leaves, forest	1	53.9	12.1	—	—
	2	63.8	7.6	—	—
	Mean	58.9 ± 7.0	9.9 ± 3.2	—	—
Twigs	1	32.9	2.5	(32.9)	(2.5)
	2	—	—	58.1	5.1
	Mean	32.9 ± 8.2	2.5 ± 1.6	45.5 ± 17.8	3.8 ± 1.8
Mean "non-Vacc. shrubs" leaves (does not include *Alnus*)		55.4 ± 13.1	9.1 ± 5.1	34.9 ± 7.1	2.0 ± 0.8
Mean "non-Vacc. Shrubs" twigs (does not include *Alnus*)		40.3 ± 17.2	3.8 ± 4.6	30.6 ± 4.9	2.3 ± 0.5
Conifers (current annual growth):					
Chamaecyparis nootkatensis	3	(47.3) ± 14.0	(1.9) ± 1.0	47.3 ± 14.0	1.9 ± 1.0
Picea sitchensis	1	39.0	4.0	—	—
	3	28.7	2.2	30.1	1.6
	Mean	33.9 ± 7.3	3.1 ± 1.3	30.1 ± 8.9	1.6 ± 0.8
Tsuga heterophylla	1	53.3	6.9	—	—
	3	31.0	2.6	26.2	1.0
	Mean	42.2 ± 15.8	4.8 ± 3.0	26.2 ± 7.7	1.0 ± 0.5
Lichens (arboreal):					
Usnea spp.	2	(71.9) ± 3.8[d]	(-2.2) ± 0.6	71.9 ± 3.8	-2.2 ± 0.6

[a] ⬚ ⬚⬚⬚⬚⬚⬚⬚ ⬚⬚⬚⬚⬚⬚ ⬚⬚⬚⬚⬚⬚⬚⬚⬚⬚⬚⬚⬚⬚⬚⬚⬚⬚ ⬚⬚⬚⬚ ⬚⬚⬚⬚⬚⬚⬚⬚⬚⬚⬚⬚⬚⬚⬚⬚⬚⬚ ⬚⬚ ⬚ ⬚⬚⬚⬚⬚ ⬚⬚⬚⬚⬚⬚⬚ ⬚⬚⬚ ⬚⬚⬚ standard deviation for class mean (e.g., "Mean Ferns") is calculated from mean (or single) values reported for each forage within the class. Standard deviations for forages with only one value (i.e., reported in only one study) are estimated by calculating the mean coefficient of variation (100 × s/x̄) for all forages with multiple values in the class and then applying that coefficient of variation to the single value to estimate its standard deviation.

[b] Data in parentheses are estimated as same values in winter as measured in summer (or vice versa).

[c] ⬚ ⬚⬚⬚⬚⬚⬚ ⬚⬚⬚⬚⬚⬚⬚⬚⬚ ⬚⬚⬚⬚⬚⬚⬚⬚ ⬚⬚⬚⬚⬚⬚⬚⬚⬚ ⬚⬚⬚ ⬚⬚⬚⬚ ⬚⬚⬚⬚⬚⬚⬚⬚⬚⬚⬚⬚ ⬚⬚ ⬚⬚ ⬚⬚⬚⬚⬚⬚⬚⬚⬚⬚⬚⬚ ⬚⬚⬚⬚ ⬚⬚⬚ ⬚⬚⬚⬚⬚ that class. The coefficient of variation for the class mean ("Mean graminoids") is applied to each of the individual ⬚⬚⬚⬚⬚⬚⬚⬚ ⬚⬚⬚⬚ ⬚⬚⬚ ⬚⬚⬚⬚⬚⬚⬚⬚ ⬚⬚⬚⬚⬚⬚⬚⬚ ⬚⬚⬚⬚⬚ ⬚⬚⬚⬚⬚

[d] ⬚⬚⬚⬚⬚⬚⬚ ⬚⬚⬚⬚⬚⬚⬚⬚⬚⬚*Usnea* ⬚⬚⬚⬚⬚⬚⬚⬚⬚⬚ ⬚⬚⬚ ⬚⬚⬚⬚⬚⬚⬚⬚⬚⬚⬚⬚ ⬚⬚⬚*Usnea* in Parker et al. 1999. Also see Robbins (1987) for digestibility of *Alectoria sarmentosa*⬚

Calculations of digestible dry matter from Parker et al. (1999) make assumption that gross energy of dry matter is a constant of 18.83 kJ/g (= 4.5 kcal/g).

Calculations of digestible protein (DP) from McClellan et al. (n.d.), and Hanley and McKendrick (1983), both of which give values of nitrogen concentration (% Nitrogen [N]) rather than DP, use the following equation, converting N to Crude Protein and then Crude Protein to DP (Hanley et al. 1992) assuming no effects of tannins:

$$DP\ (\%) = -3.87 + 0.9283\ (N \times 6.25)$$

Appendix 2: Nutritional Data (mean ± standard deviation) in the Nutritional Database *(continued)*

Sources:

McClellan et al. (n.d.): Michael McClellan, Thomas Hanley, and others at Pacific Northwest Research Station, Juneau—data from samples collected during July and August 1998, composited from several replicate sites on Prince of Wales Island as part of followup to "Second Growth Management Study." All samples, except Vaccinium leaves "from sunny habitat" were collected from shaded forest understories. Chemical analyses by Habitat Analysis Laboratory, Washington State University, Pullman. Dry Matter Digestibility estimated from fiber analysis and equation in Hanley et al. 1992. Digestible Protein estimated from crude protein (N × 6.25) and equation in Hanley et al. 1992. No values account for effects of tannins. Lower DP of Vaccinium "from sunny habitat" reflects only lower N concentration, not the combined effect of lower N

2. Parker et al. 1999.

Hanley and McKendrick 1983.

4. McArthur et al. 1993.

Hanley et al. 1992.

Appendix 3: Plant Codes of Species in the Current (2011) Database and Their Default Values for Percentage Remaining in Winter, and Maximum Percentage in the Solution Set

Species	Common name	Plant code	Type	Percentage remaining in winter	Maximum percentage in solution set
Actaea rubra (Aiton) Willd.	red baneberry	ACRU2	Forb	0	100
Adiantum pedatum L.	northern maidenhair	ADPE	Fern	0	20
Alectoria Ach. spp.	witch's hair lichen	ALECT3	Lichen	100	100
Alnus spp. Mill. leaf	alder	ALNUS	Shrub	0	3
Angelica genuflexa Nutt.	kneeling angelica	ANGE2	Forb	0	100
Andromeda polifolia L. leaf	bog rosemary	ANPO_L	Shrub	0	2
Andromeda polifolia L. twig	bog rosemary	ANPO_T	Shrub	100	2
Aquilegia formosa Fisch ex DC.	western columbine	AQFO	Forb	0	100
Aruncus sylvester Kostel. ex Maxim.	bride's feathers	ARSY2	Forb	0	100
Athyrium filix-femina L. Roth	common ladyfern	ATFI	Fern	0	10
Blechnum spicant (L.) Sm.	deer fern	BLSP	Fern	100	20
Bromus sitchensis Trin.	Alaska brome	BRSI	Graminoid	0	100
Carex deweyana Schwein.	Dewey sedge	CADE9	Graminoid	0	100
Carex lyngbyei Hornem.	Lyngbye's sedge	CALY3	Graminoid	0	100
Carex mertensii Prescott ex Bong.	Merten's sedge	CAME6	Graminoid	0	100
Carex L. spp.	sedge	CAREX	Graminoid	0	100
Chamaecyparis nootkatensis (D. Don) Spach CAG[a]	Alaska cedar	CHNO	Tree	100	100
Circaea alpina L.	small enchanter's ▯▯▯▯▯▯▯▯	CIAL	Forb	0	100
Claytonia sibirica L.	Siberian springbeauty	CLSI2	Forb	0	100
Coptis aspleniifolia ▯▯▯▯▯	▯▯▯▯▯▯▯▯▯▯▯▯▯▯▯	▯▯▯▯	▯▯▯▯	▯▯▯	▯▯▯
Cornus canadensis L.	bunchberry dogwood	COCA13	Forb	100	100
Coptis trifolia (L.) Salisb.	threeleaf goldthread	COTR2	Forb	100	100
Deschampsia cespitosa (L.). ▯▯▯▯▯▯	tufted hairgrass	DECA18	Graminoid	0	100
Dryopteris dilatata auct. non (Hoffm.) Gray	spreading woodfern	DREX2	Fern	10	20
Dryopteris expansa (C. Presl.) ▯▯▯▯▯	spreading woodfern	DREX2	Fern	10	20
Drosera rotundifolia L.	roundleaf sundew	DRRO	Forb	0	100
Elymus arenarius L.	sand ryegrass	LEAR11	Graminoid	0	100
Empetrum nigrum L. leaf	black crowberry	EMNI_L	Shrub	100	3
Empetrum nigrum L. twig	black crowberry	EMNI_T	Shrub	100	1
Epilobium angustifolium L.	fireweed	CHANA2	Forb	0	100
Epilobium ciliatum Raf.	fringed willowherb	EPCI	Forb	0	100
Equisetum arvense L.	field horsetail	EQAR	Forb	0	100
Equisetum pratense Ehrh.	meadow horsetail	EQPR	Forb	0	100
Equisetum L. spp.	horsetail	EQUIS	Forb	0	100
Fauria crista-galli (Menzies) Makino	deercabbage	NECR2	Forb	0	100

Appendix 3: Plant Codes of Species in the Current (2011) Database and Their Default Values for Percentage Remaining in Winter, and Maximum Percentage in the Solution Set *(continued)*

Species	Common name	Plant code	Type	Percentage remaining in winter	Maximum percentage in solution set
Gallium kamtschaticum Steller ex Schult.	boreal bedstraw	GAKA	Forb	0	100
Galium trifidum L.	threepetal bedstraw	GATR2	Forb	0	100
Galium L. spp.	bedstraw	GALIU	Forb	0	100
Gaultheria shallon ▢▢▢▢ ▢▢▢	▢▢▢▢	▢▢▢▢	▢▢▢▢▢	▢▢▢	▢▢▢
Gaultheria shallon ▢▢▢▢ ▢▢ ▢▢	▢▢▢▢	▢▢▢▢	▢▢▢▢▢	▢▢▢	▢▢▢
Gentiana douglasiana Bong.	swamp gentian	GEDO	Forb	0	100
Geocaulon lividum (Richardson) ▢▢▢▢▢▢	false toadflax	GELI2	Forb	0	100
Geranium erianthum DC.	woolly geranium	GEER2	Forb	0	100
Geum macrophyllum Willd.	largeleaf avens	GEMA4	Forb	0	100
Goodyera oblongifolia Raf.	western rattlesnake ▢▢▢▢▢▢▢	GOOB2	Forb	0	100
Gymnocarpium dryopteris (L.) Newman	western oakfern	GYDR	Fern	0	20
Heracleum lanatum Michx.	common cowparsnip	HEMA80	Forb	0	2
Impatiens noli-tangere L.	western touch-me-not	IMNO	Forb	0	10
Kalmia polifolia Wangenh. leaf	bog laurel	KAPO_L	Shrub	0	3
Kalmia polifolia Wangenh. twig	bog laurel	KAPO_T	Shrub	100	3
Ledum palustre L. leaf	marsh Labrador tea	LEPA11_L	Shrub	100	3
Ledum palustre L. twig	marsh Labrador tea	LEPA11_T	Shrub	100	3
Listera cordata (L.) R. Br.	heartleaf twayblade	LICO6	Forb	0	100
Listera R. Br. spp.	twayblade	LISTE	Forb	0	100
Luzula parviflora (Ehrh.) Desv.	smallflowered woodrush	LUPA4	Graminoid	0	100
Lysichiton americanus Hulten & H. St. John	American skunkcabbage	LYAM3	Forb	0	100
Maianthemum dilatatum (Alph. Wood) Mac.	false lily of the valley	MADI	Forb	0	100
Menziesia ferruginea Sm. leaf	rusty menziesia	MEFE_L	Shrub	0	100
Menziesia ferruginea Sm. twig	rusty menziesia	MEFE_T	Shrub	100	100
Mitella pentandra Hook.	fivestamen miterwort	MIPE	Forb	0	100
Moehringia L. spp.	sandwort	MOEHR	Forb	0	100
Moneses uniflora (L.) A. Gray	single delight	MOUN2	Forb	100	100
Oplopanax horridum (Sm.) Miq. leaf	devilsclub	OPHO	Shrub	0	100
Osmorhiza purpurea (Coult. & Rose) Suksd.	purple sweetroot	OSPU	Forb	0	100
Osmorhiza Raf. spp.	sweetroot	OSMOR	Forb	0	100
Oxycoccus microcarpos Turcz. ex Rupr.	small cranberry	VAOX	Shrub	0	100
Parnassia fimbriata K. D. Koenig	fringed grass of ▢▢▢▢▢▢▢	PAFI3	Forb	0	100

Appendix 3: Plant Codes of Species in the Current (2011) Database and Their Default Values for Percentage Remaining in Winter, and Maximum Percentage in the Solution Set *(continued)*

Species	Common name	Plant code	Type	Percentage remaining in winter	Maximum percentage in solution set
Picea sitchensis (Bong.) Carriere □□□[a]	Sitka spruce	PISI	Tree	100	1
Platanthera dilatata (Pursh.) Lindl. ex Beck	scentbottle	PLDI3	Forb	0	100
Polystichum braunii (Spenner) □□	Braun's hollyfern	POBR4	Fern	100	20
Potentilla L. spp.	cinquefoil	POTEN	Forb	0	100
Prenanthes alata (Hook.) D. Dietr.	western rattlesnakeroot	PRAL	Forb	0	100
Renunculus L. spp.	buttercup	RANUN	Forb	0	100
Ranunculus uncinatus D. Don ex G. Don	woodland buttercup	RAUN	Forb	0	100
Ribes bracteosum Douglas ex Hook. leaf	stink currant	RIBR_L	Shrub	0	10
Ribes bracteosum Douglas ex Hook. twig	stink currant	RIBR_T	Shrub	100	10
Ribes laxiflorum Pursh. leaf	trailing black currant	RILA3_L	Shrub	0	100
Ribes laxiflorum Pursh. twig	trailing black currant	RILA3_T	Shrub	100	100
Ribes L. spp. leaf	current	RIBES_L	Shrub	0	100
Ribes L. spp. twig	currant	RIBES_T	Shrub	100	100
Rubus chamaemorus L. leaf	cloudberry	RUCH_L	Shrub	0	100
Rubus chamaemorus L. twig	cloudberry	RUCH_T	Shrub	100	100
Rubus parviflorus Nutt. leaf	thimbleberry	RUPA_L	Shrub	0	100
Rubus parviflorus Nutt. twig	thimbleberry	RUPA_T	Shrub	100	100
Rubus pedatus Sm.	strawberryleaf raspberry	RUPE	Forb	100	100
Rubus spectabilis Pursh. leaf	salmonberry	RUSP_L	Shrub	0	100
Rubus spectabilis Pursh twig	salmonberry	RUSP_T	Shrub	0	100
Salix L. spp. leaf	willow	SALIX_L	Shrub	0	100
Salix L. spp. twig	willow	SALIX_T	Shrub	100	100
Sambucus racemosa L. leaf	red elderberry	SARA2_L	Shrub	0	100
Sambucus racemosa L. twig	red elderberry	SARA2_T	Shrub	0	100
Stellaria crispa Cham. & Schltdl.	curled starwort	STCR2	Forb	0	100
Streptopus amplexifolius (L.) DC.	claspleaf twistedstalk	STAM2	Forb	0	100
Streptopus Michx. spp.	twistedstalk	STREP3	Forb	0	100
Streptopus roseus Michx.	twistedstalk	STRO4	Forb	0	100
Streptopus streptopoides (Ledeb.) Frye & Rigg	small twistedstalk	STST3	Forb	0	100
Thelypteris phegopteris (L.) □□□□□□	long beechfern	PHCO24	Fern	0	100
Thuja plicata Donn ex D. Don □□□[a]	western redcedar	THPL	Tree	100	100
Tiarella trifoliata L.	threeleaf foamflower	TITR	Forb	100	100

Appendix 3: Plant Codes of Species in the Current (2011) Database and Their Default Values for Percentage Remaining in Winter, and Maximum Percentage in the Solution Set *(continued)*

Species	Common name	Plant code	Type	Percentage remaining in winter	Maximum percentage in solution set
Tolmiea menziesii (Pursh.) Torr. & A. Gray	youth on age	TOME	Forb	0	100
Trientalis latifolia Hook.	broadleaf starflower	TRBOL	Forb	0	100
Trisetum cernuum Trin.	tall trisetum	TRCA21	Graminoid	0	100
Trisetum Pers. spp.	oatgrass	TRISE	Graminoid	0	100
Tsuga heterophylla (Raf.) Sarg. □□□[a]	western hemlock	TSHE	Tree	100	15
Tsuga mertensiana (Bong.) □□IIIIII□□□[a]	mountain hemlock	TSME	Tree	100	10
Urtica dioica L.	stinging nettle	URDI	Forb	0	1
Vaccinium alaskaense Howell leaf	Alaska blueberry	VAOV_L	Shrub	0	100
Vaccinium alaskaense Howell twig	Alaska blueberry	VAOV_T	Shrub	100	100
Vaccinium cespitosum Michx. leaf	dwarf bilberry	VACA13_L	Shrub	0	100
Vaccinium cespitosum Michx. twig	dwarf bilberry	VACA13_T	Shrub	100	100
Vaccinium L. spp. evergreen leaf	blueberry	VACCI_L	Shrub	100	100
Vaccinium L. spp. evergreen twig	blueberry	VACCI_T	Shrub	100	100
Vaccinium ovalifolium Sm. leaf	oval-leaf blueberry	VAOV_L	Shrub	0	100
Vaccinium *ovalifolium* Sm. twig	oval-leaf blueberry	VAOV_T	Shrub	100	100
Vaccinium parvifolium Sm. leaf	red huckleberry	VAPA_L	Shrub	0	100
Vaccinium parvifolium Sm. twig	red huckleberry	VAPA_T	Shrub	100	100
Vaccinium uliginosum L. leaf	bog blueberry	VAUL_L	Shrub	0	100
Vaccinium uliginosum L. twig	bog blueberry	VAUL_T	Shrub	100	100
Veratrum viride Aiton	green false hellebore	VEVI	Forb	0	2
Viola glabella Nutt.	pioneer violet	VIGL	Forb	0	100
Viola L. spp.	violet	VIOLA	Forb	0	100
Other fern	other fern	XFERN	Fern	0	20
Other forb	other forb	XFORB	Forb	0	100
Other graminoid	other graminoid	XGRAM	Graminoid	0	100
Other shrub leaf	other shrub leaf	XSHRUB_L	Shrub	0	100
Other shrub twig	other shrub twig	XSHRUB_T	Shrub	100	100

[a] CAG = current annual growth.
Source: PLANTS Database http://plants.usda.gov/ by genus; plant code = "symbol."

Glossary

animal day (or deer day)—One animal of specified species, age, sex, and body weight for 1 day; used in Forage Resource Evaluation System for Habitat (FRESH) to quantify the food resources necessary to meet the nutritional requirements, as specified for the analysis. For deer days, we usually use an adult female as the animal; the body weight and nutritional requirements differ with season and reproductive status (see table 1). Gestation or lactation (reproductive) requirements are included in the adult female's requirement as specified in the analysis. Animal days can be one animal for several days, several animals for 1 day, or any combination thereof; however, nutritional requirements and food availability and quality are assumed constant at the time of their measurement (i.e., do not change with number of days).

carrying capacity—The capacity of a habitat's food resources to meet the requirements of a given animal species, measured in units of animal days. Note that our definition does not involve any consideration of overgrazing, plant-herbivore feedback loops, and long-term sustainability. It is an instantaneous measure of the relation between available food resources and specified animal nutritional requirements. It is best considered an index of the combination of food quantity and quality relative to the animal in question. It provides a quantitative comparison of different habitats (or landscapes) at the same time or the same habitat at different times. It is not intended as an estimate of the actual number of animals that a habitat can support on a long-term basis.

current annual growth—Leaves, twigs (shrubs), stems (herbs), and flowers and fruits produced by plants during the current growing season; the standing crop of aboveground net primary productivity exclusive of radial wood increment to the older (greater than current year) stems of woody plants. Measures of current annual growth are in terms of biomass (see below) and may include an unmeasured effect of herbivory. Current annual growth of plants in winter is the biomass produced in the immediately preceding growing season.

digestible energy—The energy in a food that becomes available to an animal upon digestion, measured in terms of kilojoules (or kilocalories) per gram ovendry weight (see below). Gross energy is the total energy in a food, as measured by combustion; digestible energy is that fraction of the gross energy that becomes available to the animal by the process of digestion. Further losses of energy include urinary and gaseous losses (the conversion of digestible energy to metabolic energy) and heat losses in chemical and mechanical work (metabolic energy to net energy), which are assumed as constant coefficients in our recommended metabolic requirements.

Digestible energy can be measured by multiplying gross energy (determined by combustion) by the dry matter digestibility (percentage) of the food.

digestible protein—The protein in a food that becomes available to an animal upon digestion, measured in units of grams ovendry weight (see below). The digestible protein concentration of a food is the digestible protein expressed as a percentage of the ovendry weight of the food. A daily digestible protein requirement can be quantified in units of grams per day or percentage of diet (for a given total daily dry matter intake). Crude protein (which equals total nitrogen times 6.25) is a measure of a food's protein content exclusive of its digestibility. Although digestible protein is highly correlated with crude protein in tannin-free grasses and agricultural legumes, it can be reduced greatly in native forages consumed by deer, especially those containing tannins (see below). In terms of nutritional requirements and food quality, digestible protein is always the better metric than crude protein.

feedback loops—Feedback loops refer to "information" feedback whereby a cause generates an effect that in turn affects the original causal factor. Positive feedback loops result in the effect increasing with time, whereas negative feedback loops result in a dampening of effect with time. The FRESH system does not account for herbivore-plant feedback loops because its calculations are based on the total ▢▢▢▢▢▢ ▢▢▢ ▢▢▢▢▢▢▢▢▢▢▢▢▢ ▢▢▢ ▢▢▢▢▢▢▢ ▢▢▢▢ ▢▢▢ ▢ ▢▢▢ ▢▢▢▢▢▢ ▢▢ included in the solution set (other than the limits imposed by the nutritional or palatability constraints).

metabolic requirements—Metabolism is the complex of physical and chemical processes occurring within a living cell or organism that are necessary for the maintenance of life. Although metabolic requirement usually refers to the daily minimum requirement for energy (see digestible energy above), we also include the daily requirement for digestible protein in our use of the term. It could include requirements for other nutritional factors as well.

ovendry weight—Weight (grams or kilograms) of a given material after it has been dried to a constant weight in an oven at specified temperature. Plant tissue is dried at various temperatures for various reasons (e.g., laboratory analyses usually require cooler temperatures than biomass determinations), but a subsample of the material is usually dried at 100 °C as a standard. If no temperature is specified with the ovendry weight, then drying to constant weight at 100 °C may be assumed. This ▢▢▢▢▢▢▢▢▢ ▢▢▢ ▢▢▢▢▢▢▢▢▢▢▢▢ ▢▢▢▢▢▢▢ ▢▢▢▢▢▢ ▢▢▢▢▢▢ ▢ ▢▢▢▢▢ ▢ ▢▢▢▢▢▢▢▢▢ ▢ ▢▢▢▢▢

biomass—The ovendry weight of plant material (grams or kilograms), often expressed on a per-area basis as biomass density (grams per square meter or kilograms per hectare). "Available" plant biomass in FRESH refers to the plant biomass that is available to deer, either by simply being physically present or above snow in winter (plant biomass beneath snow is assumed to be unavailable). Plant biomass may refer to a specific forage (species and part) or to the total of all forages, depending on context.

plant phenology—Cyclic biological events in plants, such as the seasonal changes that occur with new leaf production, maturation, flowering, fruiting, leaf-fall, etc.

plant secondary chemistry (and secondary compounds)—The study of plant chemistry dealing with compounds that are not primarily involved in the processes of growth and reproduction. Secondary compounds are those compounds that are "secondary" to basic plant metabolism and, therefore, are either secondary byproducts of metabolism, precursors or regulators of primary metabolism, or are produced for other purposes (e.g., protection from ultraviolet radiation). Many secondary products are believed to serve as protection against herbivores, either as toxic poisons or as digestibility reducing substances. Plant secondary chemistry is a very broad and complex science, as secondary compounds are virtually

tannins—A highly diverse biochemical group of various soluble, astringent, complex, phenolic substances of plant origin. Tannins are widespread in occurrence in natural vegetation, especially in woody species commonly eaten by deer. Many (but not all) tannins chemically bind with proteins to form insoluble complexes resistant to digestion, thereby reducing the digestible protein content of a forage. Because of the enormous variety of tannins and their effects, however, it is most useful to measure tannin astringency (capacity for binding a standard protein) rather than tannin concentration when evaluating forage quality for herbivores.